5, 7-9, 12

CITIES

Also available in the Small Guides to Big Issues

Climate Change
Melanie Jarman

Women's Rights
Geraldine Terry

Small Guides To Big Issues

Jeremy Seabrook

CITIES

Fernwood Publishing
Halifax and Winnipeg

Pluto Press
London • Ann Arbor, MI

macmillan

Oxfam

JACANA

First published 2007 by Pluto Press, 345 Archway Road, London N6 5AA, UK
    and 839 Greene Street, Ann Arbor, MI 48106, USA. www.plutobooks.com
Published in Australia by Palgrave Macmillan Publishers Australia, Claremont
    Street, South Yarra 3141, Australia. Associated companies and representatives
    throughout the world. Visit our website at www.macmillan.com.au
Published in Canada by Fernwood Publishing, Site 2A, Box 5, 32 Oceanvista Lane,
    Black Point, Nova Scotia, B0J 1B0 and 324 Clare Avenue, Winnipeg, Manitoba,
    R3L 1S3. www.fernwoodpublishing.ca
Published in South Africa by Jacana Media (Pty) Ltd, 10 Orange Street,
    Sunnyside, Auckland Park 2092, South Africa, tel +2711 628 3200.
    See a complete list of Jacana titles at www.jacana.co.za

Published in association with Oxfam GB

The views expressed are those of the author, and not necessarily those of the
publishing organisations.

ISBN   978 0 7453 2308 4 (Pluto hardback)
ISBN   978 0 7453 2307 7 (Pluto paperback)
ISBN   978 1 4202 5603 1 (Palgrave Macmillan)
ISBN   978 1 55266 249 6 (Fernwood)
ISBN   978 1 77009 379 9 (Jacana)

British Library Cataloguing in Publication Data. A catalogue record for this book
is available from the British Library

Library of Congress Cataloging in Publication Data applied for

National Library of Australia cataloguing in publication data applied for

Library and Archives Canada Cataloguing in Publication
Seabrook, Jeremy, 1939-
    Cities / Jeremy Seabrook.
(Small guides to big issues)
Includes bibliographical references.
ISBN 978-1-55266-249-6
    1. Sociology, Urban. I. Title. II. Series.
HT151.S43 2007   307.76   C2007-903295-8

10 9 8 7 6 5 4 3 2 1

Designed and produced for Pluto Press by Curran Publishing Services, Norwich

Printed and bound in India

Contents

Series Preface

Facts, opinions, and ideas in the fight to end poverty

Small Guides to Big Issues is a series of accessible introductions to key current global challenges.

Books in this series raise bold questions about the global economic and political system, and about how it works. They set out what needs to happen in order to end poverty and injustice. They are designed for campaigners and activists, for students and researchers, in fact for anyone interested in looking behind the headlines.

Each book is informed by personal knowledge and passion and is written in an accessible and thought-provoking style. Each book provides a critical survey of its subject and a challenging look at current trends and debates. Authors explain the global institutions and processes involved, and tackle key issues of poverty reduction, human rights and sustainable development.

The books contain case studies, analysis, and testimony from activists and development practitioners, many drawing on Oxfam's experience of working with partner organisations in more than 70 countries. Oxfam is supporting this series by asking writers with a personal on-the-ground knowledge of the issues to share their view of the key debates in each subject.

Oxfam GB

Oxfam GB, founded in 1942, is a development, humanitarian and campaigning agency working with others worldwide to find lasting solutions to poverty and suffering. Oxfam GB is a member of Oxfam International, a confederation of 13 organisations around the world working for an end to injustice and poverty. Oxfam is committed to making poverty-focused information and analysis of global issues more widely available, and is working in partnership with Pluto Press on this series in order to contribute to current debates. For clarity, the books in this series do not differentiate between Oxfam International or Oxfam GB, or regional offices or affiliate organisations – choosing rather to use 'Oxfam' to cover any or all of these institutions.

Pluto Press

Pluto Press is an independent, progressive, London-based publisher specialising in books on politics and across the social sciences that offer a radical counterpoint to the mainstream. Recent titles address some of the most pressing and contentious issues today, including the economic and ecological impact of globalisation, global insecurity and terrorism, and international human rights.

List of Boxes

List of Abbreviations

COHRE	Centre on Housing Rights and Evictions
IIED	International Institute for Environment and Development
IMF	International Monetary Fund
NAFTA	North America Free Trade Agreement
NGO	non-government organisation
SEWA	Self Employed Women's Association (India)
SPARC	Society for Promotion of Area Resource Centres (Mumbai)
WTO	World Trade Organization

Introduction

This book is concerned with the prodigious growth – both actual and forecast – of urban centres in the South. Many of the predictions, including those of the United Nations Human Settlements Programme's 2003 publication, *The Challenge of Slums*,[1] echo the apocalyptic warnings that accompanied the unplanned development of manufacturing towns and cities in the early industrial era in Britain and elsewhere. And indeed, many of these warnings were subsequently justified – living conditions in the cities of early Victorian England deprived people of basic needs, of adequate nutrition, health care and livelihood. Only by consistent agitation for government intervention and reform were these circumstances at length improved, not least because of the organisation and efforts of the people themselves.

Rapid urbanisation into cities with hopelessly inadequate infrastructure is perhaps the greatest of the transformations of globalisation. This leads to congestion, overcrowding, insecurity, sickness, absence of basic services, unemployment, and perhaps most ominous of all, the disaffection of large youthful populations, who have little hope of achieving the promises held out by the imagery of globalisation, of universal wealth and well-being.

Today we are living through an experience similar to that of nineteenth-century Britain, but the scale is world-wide. There is, however, one significant difference from the urbanisation of Victorian Britain. The global prescriptions for the squalor of urban slums are the very opposite of those that were – reluctantly but inevitably – accepted in nineteenth-century Europe. Governments now, far from intervening to regulate hours of work, public health and housing standards, have adopted policies of liberalisation and privatisation, a loosening of controls, a weakening of the powers of national governments. Instead of the State ensuring the basic needs of people are met, this is being entrusted to private interests – the very institutions that had contributed to the well-documented miseries of the unfettered free market.

This book looks at the *integration* of cities into the global economy, and asks whether the *disintegration* of cultures and societies, which accompanies it, is being adequately addressed by international institutions, governments and non-government organisations.

Urbanisation is a complex and intricate process. It brings a mixture of gain and loss, both material and psychological. It privileges certain groups and disadvantages others at different times. It affects people differently at various moments of the life-cycle: the young and vigorous are, in particular, more able to use its opportunities than the elderly or those with disabilities. Women bear a disproportionate part of the burden of humanising life in what are often degrading and damaging conditions.

The urban poor are not a homogeneous group: as well as people working at the limits of human endurance, there are also those who survive on their wits or by being part of criminal gangs. There are no generalisations to be made that do not immediately bring to mind examples of the opposite. The city is the site both of life-transforming possibilities and of extreme oppression. It is a destination of perpetual hope and optimism, even though it also takes a relentless tribute of human sacrifice.

This book takes as its starting point the assessment of the United Nations in *The Challenge of Slums,* and deals with the following issues. Chapter 1 looks at 'An urbanising world', considering the fading distinction between 'rural' and 'urban.' It explores the 'migration' of poverty from the country to the city, the phenomenon of rich and poor cities, and the asymmetry of the global economy as it is reflected in the cities of the world. Chapter 2 makes some comparisons between cities past and present, looking both at the past of cities and cities of the past. Chapter 3 explores global networks: the variable rate at which cities integrate into the global economy. It examines the concept of the 'global city', looking at several specific examples, including a place where the North confronts the South: San Diego and Tijuana on the US/Mexican border.

Chapter 4 explores migrations and cities, including cross-border migration and labour, and in-country migration. It considers permanent and temporary migrations, and how women now dominate patterns of migration in the world. Chapter 5 looks at the related issue of the urban poor, exploring the spectre of poverty, and how this is used by different political ideologies. Are the poor a reservoir of hope or the harbingers of social breakdown?

Chapter 6 goes on to consider the homes of the poor: slums, their significance and diversity. It looks at the variety of their structures, and their relationship to security and health. Issues considered include the multiple insecurities of slums, the constant threat of evictions and the wide range of different forms of tenure.

In Chapter 7 on 'Livelihoods', the core distinction is between the 'formal' and 'informal' economy. The first implies steady and regular employment, while the latter means people must find, create or make their own work. They are self-employed and often under-employed. The chapter looks at some dominant sectors of employment in the South: domestic labour, garment factories, vending, recycling, the work of street children and sex workers. There is also a large area of shadow-work, involving piracy, counterfeiting and the selling of transnational products of all kinds.

Chapter 8 considers 'Cities of fear', and how they derive from the growing gulf between the rich and poor. It looks at cities with violent subcultures, and slums dominated by 'slum-lords' and violent gangs. In these cities crime threatens stability; fires destroy the slums. The chapter explores violence against women, and extortion by police and the military. People are driven out of their minds in these conditions, and the chapter also considers mental health in cities.

Chapter 9 goes on to consider the wider provision of services, such as education, health care, water, electricity, waste removal and security. Specific issues and examples considered include the community self-provisioning of care for AIDS orphans, the issue of water: privatisation and over-use, the case of Mexico City, and the 'smell' of development.

Chapter 10 is concerned with city borders: how areas, villages and agricultural land adjacent to the city are absorbed. It explores the friction between urban and rural people. It looks at how these areas help feed the city, using the example of Hanoi; at what happens when villages become part of the urban area, taking Lucknow as an example, and at how the border area is used as dumping-ground when slums in the central city are cleared, considering in particular Bakerwala in Delhi.

Chapter 11 sets the city in a wider context by exploring rural–urban linkages. It looks at how city markets depend upon the immediate hinterland, at small urban centres, and at urban farmers in Lagos, Addis Ababa and Havana. It considers the effect of small-town urbanisation in Angola and Mozambique, and how provincial towns echo and avoid the qualities of city life.

Chapter 12 looks at a more successful side of city life: the 'triumph of the middle class'. It examines the growth of well-to-do suburbs and cities, gated communities and enclaves of luxury. It considers the privatisation of transport, and the implications of the spread of car ownership for cities. The triumph of individualism is contrasted with the conscience of the middle class. Examples are given of cities of success, like Porto Alegre and Bangalore.

My conclusion returns to the theme of how the cities of the South today replicate with uncanny precision the urban landscapes of early industrial Britain, and considers obstacles to their likely development in the image of the Western city.

Acknowledgements

This book has been influenced by the work of many writers, including most notably Lewis Mumford, Ivan Illich and Leopold Kohr. I am grateful to David Satterthwaite for introducing me to the work of the International Institute on Environment and Development, especially the research bulletin *Environment and Development*. I have been moved by the work of Carole Rakodi on the city in Africa, and Gordon McGranahan and his colleagues' *The Citizens at Risk*.[2] Although I have quoted from their work, all opinions expressed are my own.

I should like to express my gratitude to Oxfam, especially to Ranjit Ambastha and the team in Lucknow, India. I am indebted to Nikki van der Gaag for her help in organising an excess of material. I should like to express my gratitude to Gurbir Singh, P. Sebastian and the late Anna Kurien, and other members of Nivara Hakk, the people of Sanjay Gandhi Nagar in Malad East in Mumbai, many of whom I have now known for almost a quarter of a century, to Bharat Dogra in Delhi, Anita Ratnam and Solly Benjamin in Bangalore, and to the work of Sarai in Delhi.

If there is a bias towards Indian examples in the book, this is not only because this is the country I know best, but also reflects the fact that three of the world's ten biggest cities – Mumbai, Kolkata and Delhi – are now in India.

Some parts of the text have previously appeared in the *Guardian* in the UK, the *Statesman* in Kolkata and *Third World Resurgence* in Penang, Malaysia.

Jeremy Seabrook
November 2006

1
An urbanising world

No one really knows at which point a majority of the world's population will become urban. Has it already occurred? Will it happen in the next decade? In 1950, only 18 per cent of the people in developing countries lived in cities. By 2000, this exceeded 40 per cent, and the numbers continue to rise.

In any case, the distinction between urban and rural is hard to sustain. Few areas of the world have remained closed to the influence of industrial society. Not only is agriculture more and more dominated by industrial inputs, but contemporary communications systems ensure that the imagery of the metropolis penetrates more and more deeply into the consciousness and imagination of country people everywhere.

In Asia, the spread of cities has been phenomenal, and is still accelerating. China, in particular, whose celebrated economic success has been paid for by spectacular environmental destruction and a dramatic increase in inequality, is a country where it is widely estimateed that well over 100 million people are in a state of more or less perpetual migration between country and city. In the poor world, the urban growth rate is 2.35 per cent a year, whereas in the rich world it is a modest 0.4 per cent.

Few cities are prepared for this expansion. Neither national nor local governments have planned to provide the necessary extra land, housing, water, sanitation, work and waste disposal. Legal frameworks are inadequate and defective, especially in relation to land markets, including land registry, valuation and legal instruments to make the acquisition of land easier.

UN estimates of urban growth have repeatedly exaggerated the rate of development. 'Urban' is in any case a confusing definition, for it refers not only to cities but to big towns, market towns and even industrial villages. Projections of population growth in developing countries also serve as a diversion from the consumption and waste-generation rates of the rich world. In 1979 the United Nations predicted that by 2000 the population of Mexico City would be 31.6 million, of Sao Paulo 26 million and of Kolkata 20 million. Extrapolations from the recent past ignore social and economic change: the deindustrialisation of both Sao Paulo and Kolkata was not foreseen. In China, rapid urbanisation took place from 1949–60, but the cultural revolution deurbanised the country, as people were forced into new settlements. After 1977, urbanisation rose rapidly, and it has accelerated since, so that established urban settlements are being swept away to accommodate infrastructural developments and newcomers. The urban poor suffer disproportionately, especially in prestigious and capital cities: Beijing has been expanded in preparation for the 2008 Olympics, pushing migrants further from the centre.

It also became taken for granted in the 1950s and 1960s that 'urban bias' attracted people to cities: subsidised food, the availability of services and the infrastructure were seen as inducements to people to leave the countryside. It is true that average income of cities remains higher than that of rural areas, but conditions and the quality of life for some groups of urban poor are now worse than those of many rural people. It may be that a promise of wealth and the possibility of improvement draw people to urban areas, but the actual experience is often of declining health and new kinds of impoverishment.

Jorge E. Hardoy and David Satterthwaite[1] insist each city must be looked at according to its specific history and circumstances. Some cities in Africa are now growing a large proportion of their own food, and rather than the city invading the rural hinterland, the countryside is imposing itself upon the city. Lusaka and Dar es Salaam, for example, have become more, not less, self-provisioning.

Cities also die: Delhi is the site of eight former cities. Mahasthangarh, now in Bangladesh, is a ruin of a major conurbation from the first millennium before the Christian era. More than four millennia ago, the southern portion of Mesopotamia had already become 80 per cent urban in the cities of Sumeria. In 1600 Salvador/Bahia was the largest city in Brazil, when Sao Paulo was a small frontier town. Potosi, with its silver mines, was the biggest city in South America: in 1640 it had an estimated 140,000 people. The fate of cities is far from uniform – dramatic growth awaits some, and rapid collapse perhaps lies in store for others.

Towns and cities may also be destroyed. The South Asian earthquake of 2005 destroyed large parts of Muzaffarbad in Pakistan-administered Kashmir. Brigitte Overtop, an Oxfam worker, describes what she saw:

> In many streets nothing is left. Every school has collapsed. Hotels, hospitals, banks and homes have been razed to the ground. About 70 per cent of the people are homeless. There is no water and no electricity. We have to wear masks over our noses and mouths because the stench of rotting human flesh is almost too much to bear. People roam the streets dazed. Many of them are women and children. Many people came from surrounding areas to seek help.[2]

Apart from the scene of desolation, the destruction of a city of some 600,000 people illuminated how far the surrounding rural area was dependent upon the city: the life of the whole region was disrupted.

Agricultural 'improvement' is inseparable from the growth of cities: patterns of land ownership, the dominant crop or livestock, the role of intermediaries in marketing cash-crops, diversion of land to other purposes by developmental imperatives, all undermine a self-reliance which has, in any case, already been much reduced. The Green Revolution,[3] with its intensifying industrialisation of agriculture, increased productivity but impoverished many small farmers over the long term. Landholdings become more concentrated, as small-scale farmers sell their land, unable to keep up with the cost of agricultural inputs.

The need to increase agricultural exports to earn foreign exchange sets poor countries in competition with one another to produce the same products, and prices decline continuously. The dumping of subsidised agricultural goods from the North – rice, wheat, cotton – makes many local growers uncompetitive, and they quit cultivation. The compulsory purchase of land for plantations, cattle-ranches and agribusiness often leads to the employment of former subsistence farmers as wage labourers. Land reform, good agricultural productivity and agro-processing opportunities may reduce rural–urban migration, but so far the only significant reverse in the one-way traffic towards the city has been the flight of the rich from the cities, as they reclaim the peace and tranquillity of partially abandoned rural areas.

The Challenge of Slums

The most recent effort to define the likely outcome of accelerating urbanisation is the United Nations Human Settlements Programme 2003 report, *The Challenge of Slums*.[4] This shows that in 2001 924 million people (31.6 per cent of the urban population) were living in slums. In the developing world this rose to 43 per cent, while in the developed world it amounted to only 6 per cent. The report estimates that there will be 2 billion slum dwellers within 30 years 'if no firm action is taken'.

The Challenge of Slums is the most far-reaching official assessment of the implications of urbanisation. Despite the convoluted, and sometimes contradictory, diplomatic style, its overall message is clear: the 'firm action' of which it speaks means public, government or international intervention, since the growth of the kind of cities we are now seeing is a result of a global policy of unrestricted free markets, which has been rehabilitated since the fall of the Soviet Union and the decay of socialism.

The failure of governments to prioritise urbanisation leads to some dramatic, even apocalyptic, forecasts. 'Urban disaster', 'explosion', 'powder keg' and 'time-bomb' are some of the lurid images. This may be designed to inject some urgency into a debate which scarcely reaches the mainstream press in the West, but it underestimates the power of people to accommodate themselves and to create livelihoods: to find a niche in the urban economy in some of the most hostile and intractable conditions on earth. The slums are not just the sites of breakdown, violence and despair which some see. Women in particular do much to make repellent environments habitable. Human attachments, of kinship, neighbourhood and belonging, temper the worst excesses of city life, while in many places rural roots offer seasonal lifelines, and family livelihood strategies sometimes bestride both city and country occupations.

At the same time, new health problems arise in the slums. Life expectancy is lower than in the city as a whole. People are worn out prematurely by work and want, and must struggle daily for the necessities of life. This relative quietism should not be read as satisfaction with their lives; but neither should it be taken for granted that they will remain inexhaustible absorbers of the humiliations and injustices heaped upon them.

The migration of poverty

Until recently, it was generally believed that poverty was essentially an issue of the rural areas of the world. It is now clear that poverty itself is migrating with the people who have left the wasting villages and abandoned farmsteads to seek refuge in growing city slums. The rate of increase in the population in sites of urban desolation has created a new crisis, which will worsen in the next two decades: the UN forecasts that the numbers of people living in slums will grow to 2.5 billion. By 2030, rural populations will have reached their peak, and almost all subsequent population growth will be absorbed by cities.

Most people who have left the global countryside have been driven by necessity from a homeplace that may have sustained them for millennia. They have been evicted by the deteriorating productivity of the land, the cost of industrial inputs, drought, waterlogging or salination, declining prices for the commodities they produce for the market, the enclosure of agricultural land for airports, highways, resorts, or for developmental projects such as big dams or wildlife reserves.

It is one of the great paradoxes of development that people are leaving the areas where food is produced, in order that they may eat adequately. This has meant movement to urban areas, the livelihoods these generate and the markets that serve them. However, as more people arrive in the cities, many discover they have an appointment there with the very evil they are fleeing.

And for a very good reason. A dying rural tradition, made obsolete by mechanised agriculture, meets an industrial culture, which is itself obsessed with a productivity that evicts more and more people from the industrial process. Where these two epic evictions meet, city slums are formed.

Why cities grow

Migration is not the only cause of rapidly rising city populations, although historically it certainly was. Between 1551 and

1801 the death rate in London was higher than the number of births. Without continuous migration, the city would simply have perished.

Today, the natural increase of people within the city itself has become an equal factor, accounting for one-third of the growth in many urban areas. This partly reflects the youth and fertility of recent migrants. The third cause of growing numbers is the constant expansion of city boundaries: this absorbs former villages and rural areas, and also accommodates poor people dumped by authorities outside earlier city limits, as well as new middle-class settlements which have established themselves beyond the reach of pollution, overcrowding, social dislocation and crime.

There are other contributors to urban growth too. Violence, war, ethnic cleansing, religious persecution, as well as climatic disasters, earthquakes and landslides, drive large numbers of people into temporary settlements – the flimsy tents of refugees in Darfur and temporarily in Falluja – which themselves constitute the rudiments of new cities. Palestinian refugee camps have become semi-permanent slums. In Uganda, the widespread kidnapping of children pressed into the service of the Lord's Resistance Army has driven people into urban night shelters, while every year Dhaka in Bangladesh is swelled by hungry people seeking escape from the *monga* lean season. A report from Colombia in the *New York Times*[5] described the slum of La Isla:

> a kind of halfway house between an urban slum and a refugee camp. The inhabitants live as 'internally displaced persons' a term the bureaucrats use to describe refugees who stay in their own country, victims of war who were uprooted from homes elsewhere in Colombia, either by Marxist guerrillas or right-wing paramilitaries.

Box 1.1 Rural–urban – a false distinction?

The distinction between what is urban and what is rural is artificial and increasingly untenable. Many people survive by a mixture of urban and rural livelihoods. Nor is the movement between town and countryside necessarily the epic one-way journey it was in the early industrial era in countries such as Britain. Migration in Asia and Africa between the local town and the family farm, either seasonally or for a few years at a time, serves to enhance lives neither rural nor urban. Many African and south Asian cities have the aspect of an overgrown country town rather than of a major conurbation. Small plots of land on unused ground inside the city or on the periphery may well be used to grow food and reduce hunger as city populations grow. In Havana, following the decades-long US blockade, and the collapse of the Soviet Union, urban *huertos* now provide a significant proportion of the vegetables consumed in the city.

Although urban poverty is different from its rural counterpart, it is not necessarily easier. It is attended by new forms of insufficiency, insecurity and violence, unfamiliar kinds of exploitation and sickness.

Asymmetrical cities

If we understand globalisation to mean the incorporation of all the countries of the world into a single economy, it is clear that this process is occurring at a varying pace. Some countries are advantaged over others. Certain regions gain while others are bypassed. Parts of Africa are excluded, left to survive on a dwindling resource base.

Cities too present great differences in the extent to which they are absorbed into the global economy. Most Western cities have been remarkably successful, since they have long been at the centre of global economic activity. Some urban centres in the South have also adapted, specialising in industrial manufacture, finance, tourism or serving as regional headquarters of transnational companies; although this usually leaves large tracts of the city beyond the reach of formal housing markets, and devoid of services and basic infrastructure. There is a thriving central area, with its commercial and business districts, and pockets of middle-class development, but the greater part of the city is abandoned to the informal sector, where a majority of people must create their own employment.

The growth of Dubai – a materialised desert mirage – illustrates the global asymmetry. It is the largest building site on earth, employing one-fifth of the cranes in use in the world and an army of Indian and Pakistani construction workers housed in temporary barracks. More than US$100 billion is being invested in creating a metropolis of giant malls, hotels, the tallest building in the world and a series of artificial islands, a centre for trade, travel, tourism, commerce and financial services. Dubai is to be a model of what Arabia might be in the twenty-first century, a response to Western perceptions of the 'backwardness' of much of the Middle East. According to Adam Nicolson:

> this is the Dubai sandwich: at the bottom, cheap and exploited Asian labour; in the middle, white northern professional services, plus tourist hunger for glamour in the sun, and, increasingly, a de-monopolised western market system; at the top, enormous quantities of invested oil money, combined with fearsome political and social control.[6]

At the same time, the mirror-image of this is occasionally glimpsed in the rich world. The waters that swept through New Orleans in August 2005 did more than inundate a beautiful and historic city. Among the debris of buildings, stores, churches, casinos, factories and fields, human wreckage was deposited on the desolate streets – pictures of used-up humanity, the shut in and the locked away, an incarcerated populace, a concealed people, those who pay the true cost of the expensive maintenance of the American dream, intruded brutally into the sequestered dwelling-spaces of wealth.

Participants in globalisation

As cities dissolve into an increasingly amorphous countryside, the beneficiaries of globalism inhabit sites of privileged conservation. These occupy old city centres, the embalmed core, or the transformed industrial décor of warehouses and abandoned factories, or former aristocratic or merchants' dwellings. Such people are linked through networks of belonging in finance, communications, global media and discerning consumption. In one sense, they have bought themselves out of the buy-in society; they use the restaurants, concert halls and theatres of the city, and rarely meet those who have been banished to the peripheries. Indeed, such encounters are only at dangerous intersections of public transport systems, where they may occasionally run into danger from muggers, pickpockets or the drug-crazed. Much of their leisure is spent in a distant global elsewhere – the unspoiled town, the undiscovered beach, the private resort, often outside their country of origin. These city dwellers are free of the taint of the city, while still enjoying its social amenities.

The urban poor are equally participants in globalisation, but theirs can in some cases be a coercive and involuntary involvement. If a subcontractor to an international clothing company constructs a factory close to a poor suburb, it becomes the object of a kind of immense cargo cult, which may provide the residents with employment. When it relocates, they will have to fend for themselves. For most of the urban poor, survival is an individual quest; and in that respect they mirror the gilded privileged survivors in their central penthouses and 'converted' churches, lofts and industrial buildings. It would be wrong to think of rich and poor of the city as belonging to separate cultures. Both are fashioned in the image of the global market, for lives of mobility, choice and freedom. Only the poor are, to a varying extent, excluded from the opportunity to express themselves in the great hypermarkets in which global choice and freedom are located.

The networks of privilege which span the cities of the world are bound to be mimicked from below. There are transgressive networks, those involved in illegal migration, communities of squatters on public or private land, makers of pirated consumer goods or network hackers. These networks may have the potential to subvert the globalising imperative. There are also more dangerous networks set up by the urban poor: networks of crime, drugs, smuggled goods, trafficked women and children. These are caricatures of mainstream private enterprise, not detached from it, but throwing back to the dominant value-system a distorted image of itself. Cities are made up of worlds within worlds, often not touching each other and unaware of each other's existence.[7]

The city invades the countryside

The city also invades the countryside. In China, many rural areas have become dumping grounds for industrial waste. In the Huai River basin, home to more than 150 million people, the water has become too toxic to drink, with the result that liver and stomach cancer are major causes of death.[8] There are whole villages where a pervasive sickness is the 'normal' condition of the people. Refineries and smelters, quarries and mines have also been set up in rural areas, and their pollutants damage wells and watercourses. The clean-up of Beijing in anticipation of the 2008 Olympics involves transferring people and pollution away from the prestigious central areas. In Kerala, South India, in February 2004 a Coca-Cola bottling plant was ordered to cease withdrawing groundwater for four months, when villages in the Plachimada area suffered from drought and severe water shortage. Millions of young migrants to the cities of Africa have been taking the HIV virus back to their home villages, where many die, leaving their orphaned children increasingly in the care of elderly grandparents.

Even at the most elementary level, few places on earth are untouched by the imagery of global advertising: an urban-generated imagery of luxury, glamour and privilege which insinuates itself into the remotest villages. In the earth and wood homes of indigenous peoples, faded magazine cutouts of Michael Jackson, Madonna and David Beckham flutter from the walls; while in some parts of the world television sets, given as part of a dowry or bride-price, sit on tables covered with a cloth, waiting for the electricity that will summon them into vibrant, shimmering life.

The end of the city or the beginning?

Maurice Henaff suggests that at the very moment when the city is becoming global, it is ceasing to be the self-contained world which it has always been.[9] He wonders whether the decay of a coherent architectural whole, overtaken now by incontinent urban sprawl, has made the city obsolete as a productive entity. The relocation of industry world-wide, and new global technologies of communication, have overlaid older networks of streets, localities, sites of sociability and neighbourhood. Does this spell the end of the city? Or have the dispersal of production and new networks simply replicated older networks of intercourse? Are we seeing a new kind of city emerge, for which we have yet to find a form which corresponds to the monumentality of archaic cities, which embodied centralised power?

We may be in a period of transition from the monumental city to the virtual community; and this requires a rethinking of our ideas of the built environment, some aspects of which have given way to wider elective networks of affinities and sympathy. While the fabric of the city has everywhere been stretched far beyond the confines of anything recognisable as a city, the idea nevertheless remains. Its functions have simply migrated into forms which differ from those traditionally associated with 'city'. The question, according to Henaff, is how to reinvent the street and the square, the meeting place and the market, while acknowledging that older ideas of the city – as a place of familiar networks, and as a coordinated machine of production and wealth creation – have remade themselves elsewhere.

2
Cities of the past, cities of the present

The growth of cities in the South today both parallels and diverges from the urbanisation of early industrialism in Britain. There are astonishing correspondences between the conditions in which people live and lived: the picture Engels painted of nineteenth-century Manchester[1] does not differ greatly from the squalor and neglect of much of contemporary Dhaka, Kolkata and Lagos. The ingenuity of people's survival today echoes that of the child workers, hawkers, street-sellers, prostitutes and rag-and-bone men of Henry Mayhew's London in the 1850s.[2]

Although there *was* urbanisation without industrialism, especially in London and Dublin, and in Liverpool after the Irish potato famine, the cities of the nineteenth century were principally called into existence by industrialisation. The peasants who fled the impoverished countryside for pit villages or the industrial suburbs that grew around the great centres of manufacture did so because of the demand for their labour. Parts of present-day cities remind us of this. In Mirpur in Dhaka, I stood one day in a waste of huts made out of tin, polythene, *chetai*[3] and bamboo. It was dusk, and above the settlement, following the contours of the main road, were garment factories: four and five-storeyed buildings, windows white with strip lighting through the big glass windows; soaring palaces, marooned craft from another planet stranded on the edge of the slums, where garments are housed in luxurious buildings and people live in places unfit for human habitation.

The concentration of workers in the great nineteenth-century industrial cities created problems for manufacturers, not least when workers, driven by inadequate income and insecurity, formed collective organisations to win for themselves a living wage. Together with the armies of Victorian improvers and reformers, workers were effective in creating pressure for government intervention against the worst abuses. Trades unions worked, often against bitter opposition, to raise the security and wages of workers; and their efforts culminated in the West in the general establishment of the welfare state at the end of the Second World War.

Globalisation has permitted manufacturing to spread throughout the world, often deserting established industrial areas and centres of employment to seek out places where labour is cheaper. Even where there is industry, capital has sought to increase productivity by replacing human labour with sophisticated machinery. This means that the millions of people coming into the urban centres, partly because of the loss of rural jobs when agriculture becomes heavily industrialised, have created urbanisation on a vast scale, but often unaccompanied by industrial jobs. The paradox of the cities of developing countries is this: created by industrial society, they often provide little employment in the industrial sector. The reservoir of labour, indispensable to controlling wages, has become a vast ocean of people, who must secure their own livelihood outside formal structures. And at this very moment, the economic orthodoxies of neoliberalism – that government should intervene less, remove subsidies, cut spending on education, health and nutrition, indeed withdraw from economic activity – have become more insistent. The opposite of the policies that were eventually introduced to modify nineteenth-century economic conditions in Britain is now being advocated for the governance of the South. Policies that led to worsening conditions of living and working, considered intolerable in Victorian England, are now globally recommended. They are being imposed by the powerful on the industrialising countries of the South.

It is difficult to account for the moral blindness and inhumanity of this policy, which appears to its victims both arbitrary and perverse. Is it a desire to undo or to revise the troublesome history of the early industrial period, and the gains wrested by workers from those who exploited them? Is it a kind of revenge upon the lost colonial territories on which many Western countries grew rich? Is it simply the inertia of the global possessing classes who assume that 'they' must go through what 'we' did before we entered an age of affluence and prosperity? Is it laziness that cannot bear to think of the consequences for the resource-base of the planet if a whole world is remade in the image of Western society?

The ruin of peasant self-reliance

We are now seeing the globalisation of the circumstances that created industrial society in the developed world in the eighteenth and nineteenth centuries, as the sensibility of an archaic and declining peasantry was transformed into what came to be known as the working class. In seventeenth-century Britain, the rising price of cloth increased the demand for wool, and land was enclosed, removing large numbers of peasants from agriculture to make way for sheep. In eighteenth-century Britain, agricultural improvements led to a new wave of enclosures of common land by large proprietors, who claimed that production was impaired by the large number of small farmers, the system of common land and cooperative working. The enclosing landlords believed that it was a more efficient working arrangement for labourers to depend on wages and have no private interests beyond commitment to their employers. The population was increasing, people in the new industrial towns had to be fed, and the French war coincided with a period of very poor harvests. Peasants who had partly fed and clothed themselves were replaced by labourers who depended upon the farmers for wages and shops for food.

Similar beliefs echoed throughout the world in the age of imperialism, and even more insistently in the twentieth century. Peasant subsistence farmers were compelled to move into growing cash crops. The great famines of the nineteenth century perpetuated a view that the occupied lands of colonial empires were sites of constant hunger and want. The persistence of famine – in India until the 1960s, and especially in China up to the time of the Cultural Revolution – fed this image of chronic insufficiency. The conditions of self-reliance were radically altered by colonialism; and although even today many people are partly self-provisioning, few remain independent of one aspect or another of national or international markets.

The Green Revolution opened up the possibilities of unparalleled rises in productivity. It was only later that it became apparent that it led to rising costs for fertilizer and pesticides, which were required in ever greater concentrations to produce the same quantity of rice, grain or maize. With rising costs of inputs and falling commodity prices, more and more small farms were sold, so that land was concentrated in the hands of prosperous large-scale producers, and the formerly self-reliant became landless labourers. This, in turn, has fed the great migrations to urban centres.

The pace of urbanisation

Different parts of the world have become urban at a different pace and at different times. Much of Latin America was considerably urbanised before the twentieth century: in some countries, especially Uruguay, the existence of large landholdings, the *latifundia*, left little land for small-scale agriculture. Brazil experienced rapid city growth between the 1960s and

1980s, an echo of the rapid urbanisation of Germany between 1872 and 1914, during which time Germany changed from being two-thirds rural to two-thirds urban. The rate of urbanisation in Latin America has now stabilised, and with it, the intensity of slum formation, even though the cities continue to grow from within, and many millions still live in conditions of considerable deprivation.

In sub-Saharan Africa, the pace of urbanisation was rapid in the immediate aftermath of independence. Many governments tried to limit the size of towns, not infrequently through forced villagisation programmes. These activities have taken place, with a greater or lesser degree of coercion, in Tanzania, Ethiopia and Rwanda. In the past 20 years, much of the urbanisation of sub-Saharan Africa has been characterised by the chaotic growth of slums, and at the same time by an increasing tendency for family units to survive on a mixture of rural and urban livelihoods.

The growth of slums

The latest cycle in the growth of slums, and their subsequent clearance and the evictions of slum dwellers, followed the 1980s debt crisis in the South and the imposition of structural adjustment programmes by the World Bank and the International Monetary Fund (IMF). This cycle had happened many times before, although the 'clearances' were rarely on the scale seen in the last quarter of the twentieth century. Slums existed before the independence of former colonial territories. The zoning of cities by the British and French occupiers of Kenya, Côte d'Ivoire, Zimbabwe and Algeria led to clearly demarcated separate 'native quarters', and this segregation remained after the native population freed themselves from their imperial masters. The Nairobi Master Plan of 1948, for example, claimed to be based on non-segregation,

Box 2.1 Structural adjustment and hypocrisy

Mike Davis, in a splendid polemic, identifies the hypocrisy of structural adjustment policies. These demand that the developing world adopt policies (called 'reforms'), which are the very opposite of the reforms fought for by workers and the labour movement when the West was industrialising. Then, state intervention was indispensable to prevent the worst excesses of the market from destroying people's lives. Indigenous industries were protected, and services indispensable for human survival – notably the provision of clean water, sewerage and lighting and cooking fuel – were undertaken taken by public enterprise.

This was a product not of theory, but of experience. At the most utilitarian level, when the life expectancy of people in parts of industrial Manchester in the early nineteenth century was below 20 years, there was a threat that there would not be enough workers – the very reason such places existed.

The more recent neoliberal economic policies in the developed world have championed privatisation, liberalisation and opening up markets from a position of strength. This has been accomplished in the rich countries through the continuing exploitation of lands from which they had extracted their considerable colonial tribute.

It is a very different proposition to force undeveloped or developing countries to do the same thing, but this is what has been demanded by the World Bank and IMF's structural adjustment programmes. These countries have only fragile industrial development, and depend on partial subsistence or small cash-crop farming. In this context, neoliberalism is calculated to destroy indigenous development, and open these countries' markets (just as an earlier generation had opened up frontiers) to provide opportunities for Western interests.

This is seen as both injustice and hypocrisy in those places where structural adjustment programmes have ruined local production, and flooded markets with tomatoes from Italy, grain, oranges and Washington red apples from the USA, sugar from Europe, as well as soaps, chocolate, coffee, detergent and shampoo from transnational companies. Among the devastating consequences have been the deindustrialisation of Abidjan in Côte d'Ivoire, and drastic cuts in public services in Dar es Salaam and the dismantling of Nyerere's dream in Tanzania. In many parts of Africa, per capita income is lower now that it was at the time of independence.

Source: Mike Davis, *Planet of Slums*, Verso, London, 2006.

but the integration of Asians and Africans into the predominantly white districts was to be left to economic forces.[4]

Slums grew more rapidly after independence. A widely practised industrial policy of 'import substitution'[5] drew more people to cities. The Green Revolution contributed to the elimination of small farms and landholdings, and slum formation intensified in the 1960s and 1970s. It has accelerated further since the global imposition of the neoliberal ideology known as the 'Washington Consensus'.[6] In this respect, there has been continuity between the colonial and post-colonial experience.

In 1965, Leopold Kohr wrote, 'All the ancient cities flourishing to this day are in essence rehabilitated slums, created originally by paupers and slowly improved from within by their self-generated rising affluence.'[7] This ought perhaps to moderate the animosity with which the authorities in most countries of the South regard their slums; for out of them, who knows what civic strengths may one day arise?

The past of cities

Bamako

Bamako, capital of Mali, on the banks of the Niger River, was a centre of Islamic learning in the Mali Empire between the eleventh and fifteenth centuries. It fell into decline, and by the time the French occupied it in 1880, it was little more than a collection of villages covered with the dust of the searing *harmattan* wind. Mali has always been a country of migrants, in response to cyclical droughts and poverty. In the nineteenth century, migration to the peanut plantations of the Senegambia and cocoa plantations of the Ivory Coast added to a system of internal migrations. Bamako became the capital of French Sudan, and in 1924, an extension of the Dakar–Niger railway gave it communication to the sea, providing an outlet for textiles, cotton, processed meat and gold.

After independence, a series of droughts sent waves of migrants to the city in the 1960s and 1970s: in one decade, the population tripled. It is now a city approaching 1.3 million people, about 12 per cent of the country's population. It still has the aspect of a series of villages, although these have become both degraded and overbuilt.

In 1992–3 it was estimated that 47 per cent of rural families in Mali had at least one migrant member, while by 1999, more than 4 million Malians were working abroad.[8]

Sao Paulo

Sao Paulo was a small trading post in the sixteenth century, when the largest city in Latin America was Potosi, serving the silver mines of Bolivia. In the mid-nineteenth century, Sao

Paulo grew through the export of coffee, with the poorest people living in the low flood-prone areas and along the railways. The wealthy lived in substantial stone houses close to the central area of the city, but many of these declined and turned into multi-occupied *corticos* (tenement buildings), which were occupied by the urban lower middle class in the nineteenth century.

Migration from the countryside occurred on a large scale in the 1930s, as the city became increasingly industrialised. Urbanisation accelerated in the 1960s and 1970s. The 1980s saw a proliferation of *favelas,* or shanty towns on the periphery, even though this was a time of deindustrialisation, as Sao Paulo became essentially a service city. It is now the second largest urban agglomeration in the Americas, after Mexico City.[9]

Mumbai

Mumbai was a series of fishing villages on Salsette Island off the west coast of India, in the state of Maharashtra, which have, miraculously, survived along the shoreline, in spite of the growing pollution of the Arabian Sea. A minor trading post under the Portuguese, it was given to Charles II as part of the dowry on his marriage to Catherine of Braganza. The East India Company expanded trade, starting with coir and coconuts and later including betel nuts, rice, ivory, cloth and lead.

The life expectancy of colonisers was brief, as the graves in the churchyards still testify. Life in Bombay (as it was then known) was subject to cholera, malaria, typhoid and bubonic plague, outbreaks of which continued into the 1920s. Between 1896 and 1900, more than 350,000 people died of plague; older people still remember their parents' stories of fleeing the city for the shoreline during the plague, where they lived in makeshift huts until the outbreak had passed. None of this impaired the economic success of Mumbai, and it came to rival Kolkata as the second largest city of the British Empire.

In the nineteenth century, mills were constructed after the model of those in Lancashire; only within the last generation have these finally closed. The mill workers formed a radical working-class movement, which was eclipsed by the collapse of the old industrial base and the rise of the Shiv Sena Hindu communalists, part of whose programme was discouragement of non-Maharashtrian migrants into Mumbai.

The city is still marked by some splendid imperial buildings, including the magnificent Victoria Terminus, and art-deco apartments which flank the Maidan (an area of open land and playing fields in south Mumbai), but after independence, the reclamation of land in the channel divided the island from the mainland permitted the development of mid-twentieth-century skyscrapers. The magnificent horseshoe of Marine Drive still provides an exhilarating impression of space and luxury. This is deceptive, since more than half of the people of India's wealthiest city live in slums. Dharavi had the distinction of being the most extensive slum in Asia, if not the world, with its half-million inhabitants, although this may have been overtaken by Orangi in Karachi and Kibera in Nairobi.[10]

Cairo

The capital of Egypt has always been located in the metropolitan area of Cairo, although the present city was founded in the ninth century, close to the fortress of Babylon, and named *al'Q'ahira*, the Triumphant. It has always been the centre of cultivation, power and wealth of the country. Four separate settlements merged in the twelfth century to form an unified city, focus of cultural, social and economic development for the following three centuries under Mamlouk rule. By 1500, it is estimated the population was 1 million.

During the Ottoman period, the city declined and lost trade. Napoleon invaded in 1798. Three years later he was ousted by British and Turkish forces, and the city returned to Ottoman control. By 1800, the population had decreased to about one quarter of its size in 1700.

The regeneration of Cairo under Mohammed Ali (in the first half of the nineteenth century) was overtaken by the British colonisation of 1882. The old city became overcrowded and dilapidated, but elsewhere new suburbs arose in the west, north and south. It regained its 1 million population in the 1920s.

Gross inequalities led to major social and economic upheavals, and a 1952 revolt against the British and the Egyptian royal family. Vast industrial and housing projects followed in the Nasser period, and the Cairo metropolitan area had a population of 5 million by 1970. After the 1973 war, the centrally planned socialist economy gave way, and attracting international and Arab investment became the principal government objective.

By 1980 the population of greater Cairo was 8 million, and by 1994 about 12 million, with more than 4 million living in illegal settlements. This includes an unknown number living among the Mamlouk tombs in the City of the Dead, and many rooftop settlements, which have expanded from their original purpose as housing for servants in houses with flat roofs. Cairo has a population density of 100,000 per square kilometre, rivalling Mumbai in overcrowding.[11]

3
The global network

The cities of the South are differentially integrated into a global economic system, which goes forward unevenly. Vast urban areas are caught up in its vortex, as when for example a significant portion of global garment manufacture is relocated to a new country or export-processing zone. Then, when polluted areas are abandoned or cheaper labour is discovered elsewhere, many people find themselves left to their own resources. There is no forward, or planned, development. Investment is opportunistic and volatile. Efforts have been made by the international financial institutions and the WTO to adapt the economic policies of a majority of governments in the world to these uncertainties. This itself may be regarded as an invasion of national space by the forces of globalisation.

If the outcome varies from country to country, this is not because the policies and recommendations offered to governments of the developing world have been tailored to the context in which they are implemented. Rather it is because there are different cultural, social or political conditions: authoritarian governments may impose such policies more stringently. In countries with large populations, becoming a migrant may be more acceptable. (In Bangladesh and the Philippines, remittances from migrants to their families back home make up a large proportion of GDP.) Cultural characteristics may make the people of some countries more adaptable – Thailand's promotion of itself as 'a land of smiles' has made it a global centre of tourism, including the sex trade. The relationship between this insertion of the global into the national also depends upon the relationship of global institutions with 'national' authorities. The mechanisms that facilitate global integration are often state institutions, and the institutions that permit the accelerating movement of capital are sited in national territories.

Even the most nebulous of enterprises – those not rooted in a particular locality at all, such as the information industries, finance and IT – are only partly located in electronic space. They also require sites of labour, city offices and business centres, and the material resources that serve them, including infrastructure and qualified personnel. Saskia Sassen speaks of the 'collapsing temporality' of the historic hinterland of the nation-state, and the intersection of this with a new temporality of globalisation.[1] This means that similar processes are at work in time as in space, so that because of the enhanced speed of communication, information, news and events occur simultaneously, both at the point from where they are transmitted and at the sites which receive them.

How this works can be seen clearly within the cities themselves.

Cairo

Cairo contains 58 per cent of Egypt's tertiary sector (that is, administrative and service activities), two-thirds of the bureaucracy, and creates more than half of the national industrial product. Liberalisation has not led to decentralisation, only to relocation around Cairo and its ports. Greater Cairo contains 18 per cent of Egypt's people and creates 52 per cent of GDP. Egypt's second city, Alexandria, contributes less than 15 per cent of GDP.[2]

Cairo is the biggest market in the Arab world, despite the low average purchasing power of its people. The Greater

Cairo region attracts 86 per cent of foreign investment. Only Cairo has the infrastructure and competent personnel to react quickly to changes in demand, or to changes in the rules of business. There is a synergy made up of banking facilities, administration, bureaucracy, the head offices of enterprises and specialised services.

In the 1990s, the built-up area of Cairo doubled, although the city population was growing more slowly than the country generally. The growth was in two directions: on the desert fringes, in the form of new cities, industrial zones and private residential areas; and in the fertile Nile Valley, where agricultural land has been eroded by informal settlements. Earlier planning – like that of many other cities – has been overtaken by the dynamic of growth.

Economic restructuring and the dismantling of state enterprises as a result of the IMF-imposed structural adjustment programme in 1991 have transformed the city. This has resulted in the creation of industrial zones such as Six-Octobre in the western desert, and Dix-de-Ramadan to the north-east. These, planned by the state, have succeeded in attracting private investment, through ten-year tax exemptions, infrastructure, and their position on good transport axes. Six-Octobre alone produces 2.34 per cent of the total output of Egypt; of 722 enterprises, 203 have international links. (Dix-de-Ramadan produces 3.46 per cent.) This is in spite of a population of only 60,000. Most residents are lower-middle class, and commute long distances to their places of work. Close to these zones are high-class residential compounds with names like Beverley Hills, Dreamland and Park Hills. These private cities have swimming pools, golf courses, schools, hospitals and shopping centres.

At the same time the central areas of Cairo have been reconfigured, in a dual process of both growth and marginalisation. The old business quarter – overcrowded, congested, housed in dilapidated buildings – has been overtaken by areas on the West Bank of the Nile. These have taken on functions related to globalisation, especially in the service sector – the head offices of Egyptian and international enterprises, business services, consultancies, finance and banking, advertising and communications.

There has been a rise in places of consumption and leisure, dominated by international outlets – KFC, Pizza Hut, McDonald's, Subway, as well as the logos of transnationals – Benetton, Naf-Naf, Daniel Hechter, Mexx. These are located in university areas, business districts and tourist zones, and since 1995, increasingly, in malls, often associated with big hotel chains. They also appear in middle-class residential areas, and attract young people, not always to consume, but to meet and to be seen. This reflects the disappearance of public urban spaces.

But the old inner city has been degraded. The withdrawal of the state from the economy has had a dramatic impact on areas adjacent to the centre. This is conspicuous in the industrial area of Shubra al-Khayma, which became a major textile centre in the 1940s, at the heart of an integrated network of public-sector enterprises – mills providing fabric for the clothing industry. With liberalisation, the public enterprises of the textile industry were cut off from their distributors, since subsidies were removed from public distribution outlets. Foreign firms under licence raised the quality consciousness level of middle-class consumers, and there were massive lay-offs in the public sector. Many subcontractors turned to the lower end of the market, supplying restricted local outlets in the poor areas. China and Pakistan competed with Shubra al-Khayma, and the clothing industry of Six-Octobre was better equipped to deal with the challenge. Six-Octobre enterprises specialise in finished goods, and have the advantage of private national distribution networks.

There has been a double movement: the decline of the former industrial zones close to the centre, and the rise of new industrial areas. This rearrangement of intra-urban spaces is a direct result of the global integration of a dominant industry. This pattern is discernible in many established cities.

Caracas

Cities respond to a shifting global division of labour. Caracas has been buffeted by oil wealth, political turbulence, and polarisation between the middle class and the excluded. This has been thrown into sharper relief by the Leftist president, Hugo Chavez, who has aroused passionate antagonisms by his commitment to the cause of the poor. The poor have only their numbers to counter the influence and power of the possessing classes.

Caracas has expanded from a metropolitan area into a metropolitan region. This has led to territorial segregation, with the wealthy in central gated areas, and the middle class and low-income groups pushed to the periphery. Privilege is absorbed in the global economy, while the excluded are relegated to an economy of poverty. This does not consist of separate blocs of rich and poor, but of multiple fragments of unequal communities. This fragmentation dates from the 1980s, when five municipalities were created, and was intensified more recently by the establishment of an overarching municipal authority which has no jurisdiction over the city's periphery. Some of the sub-regions are separated by mountains from the city. High-income groups live in the valley of Caracas, while the peri-urban (or suburban) areas serve the poor and vulnerable middle-class groups.

The oil industry created new highly skilled jobs, but marginalised the poor, including new groups of the downwardly mobile. Construction of hotels, shopping malls, a stock exchange, offices of financial institutions and transnational companies takes place side by side with growing self-employment in a low-productivity, low-income, informal sector, as formal-sector jobs have contracted, and professional labour has been eroded.

As the city grows, it fragments and becomes multiple cities. The primary city provides areas of emblematic modernity, while vulnerable groups and the new poor are exposed to crime and violence, from which the well-off protect themselves. Middle-income households are driven to degraded parts of the city, displacing poor groups, and sometimes uncomfortably close to them. Low-income groups are locked into territorial isolation, exclusion and non-participation in the benefits of metropolitan society. Self-build squatter groups are socially homogeneous, as are privileged communities. The peri-urban area is characterised by greater social heterogeneity and becomes the site of social conflict.

The use by Chavez of Venezuela's oil wealth to relieve the poverty of the capital city is a long-term project. However effective the protests of his well-organised and vocal opponents, there is little sign that the wealthy are going to be dispossessed. For all the rhetoric, it seems that the windfall of oil riches will be applied to a somewhat more just version of the ideology that the rich must get richer if the poor are to become less poor. How radical a programme this represents is still to be seen.

World cities and non-world cities

Population and 'connectivity' are the two major indices of world cities, as defined by the Globalisation and World Cities Research group in 2002.[3] This study measured connectivity by the presence of 100 international companies in the fields of accountancy, advertising, banking and insurance, law and management consultancy, each of which has a minimum of 15 identifiable separate offices. It assessed 316 major cities using these criteria. Those cities that had at least one-fifth of the connectivity of the most connected city (London) were identified as world cities. This may be a rough and ready framework, but it gives some sense of the degree of integration into global networks.

Cities that have a population of more than 3 million, but do not make the GAWC list, were judged to be 'non-world cities'. This may because these are subordinate to an even larger city in the country which serves as a point of entry to global connectedness – Nagoya and Alexandria are big cities that do not achieve world status because they are overshadowed by Tokyo and Cairo. Such cities were removed from the list. This left eleven non-world cities which have a population of over 3 million and do not share the national territory with a world city. They include Tehran, Dhaka, Khartoum, Chongqing, Kinshasa, Lahore, Hyderabad, St Petersburg and Tianjin.

Despite their size, these cities are too poor to provide enough consumers for sophisticated international producer services. These developments cannot be described as urbanisation without globalisation, since all cities have some global connections; 'urbanisation with only basic economic globalisation' is a preferred term.

Some of these cities have undergone catastrophic decline. Khartoum and Kinshasa scarred by war and social unrest, have been abandoned or avoided by global capitalism. Others – Pyongyang and Tehran – are cities where national policies have discouraged economic connections to advanced capitalist economies. Baghdad was excluded from the global economy, first by sanctions and then by invasion and occupation. These cities may be classified into poor cities (with a small middle-class base), collapsed cities (victims of war and strife, like Kinshasa), excluded cities (Baghdad) and resisting cities (Pyongyang).

Loosely connected cities are defined as those whose degree of connectivity is less than that predicted by their population. The least connected by this criterion are Kolkata, Lagos and Karachi. They tend to be large cities in poor countries. Their population is not matched by the amount of producer service activity found in other global cities.

This provides some valuable insights. By the same judgment, it turns out that the most connected cities are London, New York, Hong Kong, Singapore, Amsterdam, Milan, Frankfurt, Madrid and Toronto. Of course, there are enclaves of transnational elites in even the most unconnected cities, whose lives tap into global circuits of wealth and power; just as in the most connected, there are areas of deprivation and impoverishment. If these isolate people from the mainstream of the country of which they are nominally a part, they remove such desolate neighbourhoods even more effectively from global networks, to which it could be argued the city is primarily oriented.

Metropolitan cities

Globalisation has the power to rearrange spatial relationships in distant cities, but this is, of course, no more than has occurred within cities in the countries of the rich industrialised world, which rearrange their spatial relationship within the so-called metropolitan area. Jacques Donzelot writes of the city in the West in general, but in France in particular, as 'a three-speed city', with three broad zones.[4] He describes these as the zones of relegation, peri-urbanisation and gentrification. The zones of relegation are home to the choiceless poor, where recent migrants and residents who are unable to get out are forced into reluctant closeness. People turn inwards, seeking security indoors, away from the public spaces, which are colonised by drug dealers, criminals and gangs. These places may be large-scale social housing schemes, within the city or on the periphery. The remoteness of them from the main city sometimes means that they form a resource for the informal and criminal sectors, providing illegal labour and trafficking in forbidden substances.

The majority have been caught up in peri-urbanisation, which, in Anglo-Saxon countries is called suburbanisation. These are people of the lower-middle and middle classes, many of whom are originally from the old inner city or social housing schemes. They are caught between fear of the stranger, the invader, the burglar and the mugger, and the forced mobility of their lives, which depend on long journeys for work, leisure and shopping. They have fled the city in search of a security which nonetheless eludes them, since they are in constant movement, sometimes spending a considerable portion of their time in traffic to and from vital destinations.

These peri-urbanites look out defensively, from behind walls and fences, locked in with the help of bolts, security lights and guard dogs. A mixture of withdrawal and mobility is a contradiction, which their relative comfort cannot reconcile. One response is to privatise public spaces, so that these are secure against predators who are believed to populate the outside. These places also buy access to schooling which will not be at risk by an influx of people from the inner city. Indeed, some suburbs see house prices rise, precisely because they form the catchment area for desirable schools. Men usually retain full-time work, but women are drawn into part-time labour, since they typically remain responsible for the family and household.

The leaders of gentrification have pioneered a sort of unofficial 'return to the city' movement. From the upper middle and professional classes, they have often chosen to 'recolonise' the old city centre, especially historic residential areas and converted warehouses, docks, factories, chapels and former sites of industrial labour. They usually live close to where they work, or work from home, often in IT, finance, the media, legal or higher medical professions. Men and women share child-raising responsibilities, and the careers of neither are seriously disrupted. Their double income ensures the maintenance of their privilege. They are constrained by neither the forced immobility of the poor quarters, nor the compulsory mobility of the suburbs. They live in the best-policed neighbourhoods, and their lives are linked to their global social kind. They may have a house in another country where they take refuge for vacations or periods of intense work. They are distant from the poor. The main risk to their security comes in metro or subway interchanges, where their trajectory briefly crosses that of the have-nots. They live globally on a local scale, and get the best of all worlds.

The North–South interface: San Diego and Tijuana

The restructuring of cities from afar is a consequence of the new emerging global division of labour. In certain regions, however, the borders between rich and poor create cities which merge economically across frontiers. A notable example is San Diego in California and Tijuana just over the Mexican border, which effectively combine the functions of both advanced and underdeveloped cities, with a metropolitan population of about 3 million. Located close to the Pacific and port facilities, with a superb climate, this is where the most powerful impact of globalisation and migration is felt along the fault-line between the industrialised and developing worlds.

Mexico is California's major trading partner, and California has more Mexico-born residents than any other US state. Shoppers from Mexico spend more than US$3 billion annually in San Diego.

Tijuana is the home to extensive *maquiladoras*: foreign-owned plants that assemble imported parts and export finished goods. They produce electronic goods, medical supplies, garments, auto parts, plastic and metal goods. The *maquiladoras* were first established in 1966 in Baja California and Ciudad Juarez. Initially, they were set up only in the border region with California, as a temporary solution to the unemployment of farm workers (*braceros*), who were no longer allowed to work in the USA. In the 1980s, following the debt crisis and the acceptance of neoliberal ideology, *maquiladoras* began to play a more significant role in the economy. They were extended throughout the country.

Wages and working conditions are as basic as might be expected; independent labour unions are not permitted. There are grisly consequences of the neglect of welfare and of the well-being of the people. In 1993, in the *barrio* (slum) of Chilpacingo, six anencephalous children were born (that is, they were born without a brain). The following year, 13 children were born with the same defect. Above the settlement there was a battery-recycling plant. Lead and heavy metal deposits were found to be in the soil at concentrations 40,000 times above safe limits.

About 2 million people live in Tijuana, the majority filling up the steep canyons and valleys that provide a natural barrier between the USA and Mexico. The chain-link fence which separated them was replaced in the early 1990s by a stronger steel-matting fence which stretches out into the Pacific Ocean, far enough to deter even the strongest swimmers from trying to circumvent it. Since Operation Gatekeeper in the mid 1990s increased border security, more than 2000 migrant deaths have been reported each year. People trying to cross into the USA are forced into mountains and deserts in the region, where they are exposed to extreme heat and dehydration. The attraction of crossing the border remains the wage differential

– in California workers can earn more in an hour than they make in a day in the *maquiladoras*.

Every year since the North America Free Trade Agreement (NAFTA) was set up in 1994, the number of *maquiladoras* in Mexico increased, until 2001 when there were 3700. Since then there has been a decline, and between 2000 and 2002 500 closed down. More than 250,000 workers lost their jobs, partly because wages, although low, had doubled in 20 years. Many companies pulling out did so in order to relocate in Asia, especially China. In June 2003 there were 3251 *maquiladoras* in Mexico, employing 1,090,000 workers. They are one of the largest sources of foreign exchange to the Mexican economy.

Companies are not required to pay local taxes in the cities where they operate, so there are no funds for infrastructure or social services, either from the government or from the companies themselves. People have to make their own arrangements for health care, housing and even garbage disposal. Women workers, who are in the majority in many factories, complain of wages below subsistence, long hours, inadequate safety and health conditions, child labour, exposure to toxic substances, pollution in the workplace and harassment of those who try to organise.

Over 5 million people pass between San Diego and Tijuana every month. More than 40 per cent of the people of Tijuana have relatives in the USA. According to the US census,[5] 27 per cent of San Diego County's population was of Hispanic origin in 2000, while 22 per cent spoke Spanish at home. It is forecast that the population of San Diego County will be more than half Hispanic by 2040.

Four major problems affecting the border region have been identified: urban sprawl, migration, racial and socio-economic segregation, and concentrated poverty, both urban and rural. In Tijuana, half of all new residents live in squatter communities, without infrastructure and with insufficient drinking water. Tijuana is a leisure destination for many young Americans, since alcohol is permitted to over-18s, as against over-21s in California. There is also a thriving sex trade. Drugs, guns and sexual violence lead to high levels of crime, family breakdown and gang rivalries. HIV rates are high – some estimates claim 60 per cent of the adult population are HIV-positive.[6]

Tijuana presents all the characteristics of a frontier city; but this only makes more concrete the reality that all the cities of the South are border cities. All are penetrated by the global economy, all have their enclaves of extreme wealth, and most have poor majorities. It is simply that, for most, the other side of the border is made visible only through television. They can see the world beyond, the attraction of a development which, although it disturbs and draws millions, also inspires hope that with time, all the people in the slums and squatter settlements will also live in the same style as those whose shadows flicker before them each day on the screen.

4
Migrants to the city

Every year, 70 million people are added to the urban population of developing countries. World-wide, however, it is estimated that about 200 million people leave their home each year in search of a livelihood – 3 per cent of the population of the earth. The great majority migrate within their own country. Of the approximately 175 million people who live outside their country of birth, 120 million are migrants. The proportion of illegal migrants is unknown. In the USA, it was estimated in March 2006 that there are up to 12 million.[1]

Each year, significant numbers of immigrants are admitted legally to the West – especially as medical personnel, as IT experts, or to service the hospitality and tourist industry. The money they earn supports whole families, even villages, in the form of remittances (that is, money sent back home). So great is the prize that people pay agents and intermediaries their life savings to reach places where their labour will be adequately rewarded. Families sell land, take children out of school, sell wedding jewellery to pay for the passage to prosperity of one member.

Maidservants from the Philippines and Indonesia in Hong Kong, Singapore and Malaysia; drivers, cooks and gardeners in Saudi Arabia; construction workers and labourers from Bangladesh, India and Indonesia in Taiwan and the Gulf; palm-oil plantation workers in Malaysia; restaurant staff all over the world; Thais and Filipinas who have gone as sex workers, escorts and lap-dancers to Japan, Europe and the

USA; nurses from the Caribbean, West Africa, the Philippines and Kerala who enhance the health services of the rich countries; miners from Lesotho and Mozambique in South Africa; young men from villages in South Asia absorbed by the have-a-nice-day culture of a global fast-food industry; Filipinos, who comprise 27 per cent of the world's seafarers; Mexican workers in seasonal fruit and vegetable harvests of the USA – these are just a few of the displaced in the global economy, which scoops up labour as easily as potatoes or apples, and whisks it round the world at the convenience of global capital.

In some countries – Gambia for instance – migrants make up one-third of the population. Remittances from the 25 per cent of migrants in the population of Côte d'Ivoire constitute one-quarter of the GDP of Burkina Faso. These are the most conspicuous people in a vast global movement of humanity. In some parts of the world, whole villages are semi-deserted, or communities of widows; in others, such as Korat in Northern Thailand, and Fujian Province in China, only the elderly and the very young remain.

Figures suggest that Bangladesh depends upon migrants for US$3 billion a year, the Philippines for US$3 billion, Sri Lanka $1 billion, Egypt $3.7 billion, and India over $11 billion. These sums are a significant underestimate, for they do not include illegals and clandestines, the forbidden migrants, without whom the global economy could scarcely function. The Central Bank of the Philippines registers more than twice the World Bank estimate of incoming funds. Remittances constitute 24 per cent of the export of goods and services from Egypt, 18 per cent of India and 14 per cent of the Philippines. This is the equivalent of 282 per cent of the total overseas assistance received by Egypt, 779 per cent by India, and 1047 per cent by the Philippines. Migrants from Latin America to the USA send home $18 billion a year; remittances make up 14 per cent of the GDP of El Salvador. In Albania, Bosnia and Herzogovina, Cape Verde,

Jamaica, Jordan, Nicaragua, Yemen and Samoa, remittances account for more than 10 per cent of GDP.

Many dynamic young people from the South are drawn to onward migration to richer cities of the earth. Their eagerness to depart, and the willingness of others to convey them to the forbidden shores of wealth, lead to the lucrative business of human trafficking; the captivity of sex workers, the bondage of domestic labour, the slavery of those whose smuggled and illegal presence permits forms of exploitation they could scarcely imagine in the places they desire so ardently to leave.

The status of migrants tends to be low. Their labour is despised when they work, as most do, in jobs that local people consider inferior. They have been overworked, often underfed, beaten and abused in dormitories and barracks in Jeddah and Kuala Lumpur; in attics in Frankfurt and Paris; in the gilded cells of massage parlours in Yokohama and New York, in damp cold rooms, where windows are stuffed with paper to keep out draughts, in the yellow-brick tenements of north London. They have shared beds with strangers on twelve-hour shifts, slept on floors and in the corridors of restaurants, on the benches beside sewing machines, in boxes stamped Bosch and Mitsubishi in the doorways of northern cities.

They have learned extremes of frugality: how to survive spending no money on themselves; walking to work, making one cigarette last all day, in canvas shoes and thin plastic coats, frayed trousers, darning their socks beneath low-watt light bulbs in unheated rooms. The money sent home has been won at the cost of isolation and self-denial, of which those for whose sake it has been suffered in silence know nothing. The consolation for returnees is their small savings, the pride of survival and tales of the wonders they have seen. Little will be told of the privations endured in hot kitchens and cold garrets, a life shared with rats and roaches, a time of servility and humiliation without end.

'Illegal' migrants

The statistics of those who have come illegally to the cities of the rich world are mostly guesswork. The numbers in Britain have been estimated at between 300,000 and 1 million. Whatever the precise figures, the life of 'clandestines' is often one of extreme exploitation. Their situation gives them no power of negotiation over any work they are offered.

Box 4.1 Suwarno

Suwarno is 22. I met him seven years ago, when he was a child worker at home in Indonesia. He has now been in Italy for 15 months. He went on a tourist visa, and simply overstayed, merging with other families from his home near Surabaya in Indonesia. He slept in the kitchen of a family living near Termini Station in Rome for the first six months, eventually finding work with a travelling clothes shop, an old van, which catered to the poorest people on the periphery of Rome. He worked 15 hours a day for 20 euros.

Someone told him Spain was giving an amnesty to illegal migrants, but he could not afford the exorbitant fare demanded by the traffickers. In any case, the amnesty was only for people who already had employment in Spain. He moved to a resort on the Adriatic, taking photographs and selling sunglasses. Since most people now have digital cameras, there is no demand for photographers. The trade in sunglasses with fake logos is not enough to create a livelihood.

Suwarno must send money home each month. No one at home knows of his condition. He has become thin and

anxious, particularly since the increased activity of the
Italian police in the wake of the London bombings of
July 2005. He dare not report his presence to the authorities. He cannot earn enough to live. Yet he cannot, will
not, admit to his family the penury and squalor in which
he lives. So powerful is the ideological pressure of the
successful migrant that he must maintain the fiction, at
no matter what cost to himself.

Life in the city

The increase in urban population in the developing world, at
least in established cities, comes from three major sources,
each contributing an approximately equal share of growth.
The first is migration. Some migrants are joining relatives,
former villagers and neighbours, who have been settled for
some time in the city. Others migrate in response to falling
farm incomes, declining productivity of land, the takeover by
the state of land required for dams, airports or roads, a dearth
of water, lack of resources to buy the inputs required for
crops, or an inability to switch to higher-value crops.

In Delhi, for example, the increase in population is still largely
fed by migration. In 1991, it was estimated that 178,000 people
migrated to Delhi. This reached 229,000 in 1996 and 241,000 in
2000.[2] This increase is more than one and a half times the natural growth of the existing population. The majority of migrants
are young. Males in the 15–34 age range come for work, while
women come primarily for marriage.

The second source of the growth of cities is the expansion
of city boundaries. This encloses former villages into the city,
and permits the construction of new suburbs, for both middle-
class escapees from the central city area and the relocated

urban poor. As the old village areas expand, some become degraded in the process, creating new slums.

The third contribution to population is accounted for by the numbers born in the city. That this is the smallest sector echoes the experience of nineteenth-century Britain: in the 1850s, up to 75 per cent of the population of Glasgow and Manchester were born elsewhere.[3]

This is a rather schematic account of urban growth, which needs qualification. Migration is no longer the epic and irreversible departure it might have been in the nineteenth century. Passing between town and country is a practical matter, an almost casual journey undertaken in a just few hours by bus, train or river launch. People are not separated irreversibly from their background, and many move easily between city and country. Journeying back to one's country of origin can also be a relatively simple affair. The ease of travel between Britain and Bangladesh makes many Bengalis in East London lead lives that have multiple roots. Some family members are in Sylhet, others in London, and they move readily between the two, with no great sense of unease or discomfort in either.

This is not to minimise the impact the city has on the imagination of new migrants. They often say they are overwhelmed. The simultaneity of things happening creates disorientation and makes them easy prey for those who recognise the country dress and manner of newcomers. Their initiation into the city is sometimes brutal. In Manila, I met a young man who (like Florence Dombey in Dickens' novel, *Dombey and Son*), was robbed of his clothes on the day he arrived in the city. He was left shoeless and in his underwear in the middle of the night. Stories are common of people who recognise the familiar accent of home, and eagerly make friends and confidants of their new acquaintances. These promise help with a lodging or a rented room, where the newcomers may be swindled, their suitcases or savings stolen.

Box 4.2 Garment workers in Bangladesh

Most migration – both casual and permanent – takes place within countries, especially poor countries, driven by economic pressure. A majority of migrants are young, and an increasing proportion are female. When I met them, Moshada, Nayantara, Rafiya, Mussamad Amina Khatoun and Ruma, aged between 12 and 14, had just arrived in Dhaka from a village near Dinajpur in North Bengal, one of the poorest parts of Bangladesh. They are part of the constantly changing population of workers in garment factories, the pool of poor young women who constantly replenish the demand for labour in the city. They were chaperoned by Mostara, 25, who was the second wife of Moshada's grandfather, so technically her grandmother.

The girls have been working a few months. They have the raw eagerness and open curiosity of country children, but are already chastened by factory life: the discipline, overcrowding, harshness of overseers, the occasional brutality. City life involves sharing dark, sometimes windowless, rooms with four or five others.

The work is from 7.30 a.m. till 6.00 p.m., but when there is an urgent export order, it continues until 10 p.m. or later. Occasionally they work all night. At such times, they are locked in. Recent spectacular fires have claimed the lives of garment workers, but this has not altered the practice. Everything depends upon delivery times.

The girls work in the same factory. They make shirts, jackets, half-pants, full pants and *genii* (T-shirts). Mostara is a machinist and quality checker. She knows the goods are exported, but does not know where. She has heard of London, but does not know where it is. Mostara earns 1,800 taka a month. The young girls earn between 1200 and 1600 taka (US$20–28).

Mostara lives with her daughter and husband, who is a rickshaw driver, not working at present because he is sick. Mostara owns two rickshaws, which she rents out at 50 taka a day, so she has an assured daily income as well as the factory wage. She says, 'The land around Dinajpur is very poor quality. Even people with land find it yields very little. I came to Dhaka two years ago, and left my brother to cultivate the land. After some time, I called Moshada, and she sent for her friends and relatives.'

The movement of people from the same community creates a sense of home; so this part of Hammond becomes a little Dinajpur, where people come and go all the time. This is a common practice in cities, where people from the same area settle, staying together, sometimes pooling non-economic resources in terms of child care, mutual help and finding work.

Moshada can read and write a little, but despite three years' schooling in the village, the others cannot. There are five people in Moshada's family. Her father is a rickshaw driver, and her mother works in a garment factory. Moshada gives her wages to her father. When she needs new clothes, she asks him and he hands money to her mother. Moshada likes the factory. She is making a contribution to her family, which gives her status. She is also part of the modern world.

> In the village, I would be working in the home or the fields. Factory work is the future. The first time I saw the factory I was very frightened. I was

shocked by the noise, the crowd, the speed. Village life is slow, here everyone is in a hurry. You get used to it. When we go home, we feel impatient, because people do not know what we are talking about. We are better than they, because we have travelled.

This is the story of many recent migrants. They would stay at home, if there was a livelihood there, but they soon become reconciled to the city. The difference between the urbanising twenty-first century and the early industrial period is that migrations today are provisional and reversible. Some women work for a few years, then return home to get married. Others get married in the city – often to cycle-rickshaw drivers or construction workers – and remain. Some alternate between city and country, going home for harvest or the rainy season, or when work is slack in the factories. The more conservative, and those with substantial economic interests in the rural area, go back home for marriage; the landless are most likely to remain.

Fractured families

Other costs are borne by migrants who take their labour to cities, internally and transnationally. These show up in no one's bottom line, since they exist in the measureless pain of separation from those they love. Children grow up without a father or mother present, receiving instead pictures of an immaculate capital city of another country, an image of skyscrapers and palm trees, and money that can never compensate for the missing tenderness and the unfelt caresses.

This is made even more tragic by the reliance of parents upon support networks of family to sustain the children. These networks become thin and frayed, worn out by changing family structures, AIDS and the ruin of subsistence.

There is the cost to spouses tired of waiting for those grown older in the service of money – women who abandon their children, men who take a second or third wife to the empty village home. What are the feelings of the children of the dancer in the Manila club, the daughter of the driver in the marble palace of Riyadh, the child of the factory worker from Fuscous? What resentments and angers grow in the spaces that separate loved ones of the same flesh and blood?

Although most new migrants to the city are young, two trends are clear. Women now outnumber men in the migrations of the world; and with increasing longevity, many older people are now coming to the city to join their children. As the elderly become more frail and unfit for field work, they seek refuge with children who left the village 20 or 30 years earlier. They are not always welcome. Even those who have grown old in the city sometimes express amazement at the unexpected indifference of their children.

Rising life expectancy leaves more and more people too frail to work until they die. In the past, those who wasted away slowly or suffered lingering illnesses were relatively few, and extended families were able to look after them. Now, with smaller families, more old people, increased mobility and urbanisation, this is ceasing to always be the case, although there are many instances of families that survive very difficult circumstances and remain close and mutually supportive.

Many older people who have left the village are disappointed by their children's failure to support them adequately. Older women pay a heavy price for female longevity, since they continue to work and contribute to the family income.

Box 4.3 Family life in Firebaugh

In Firebaugh, west Delhi, many elderly people have come to seek the protection of their children. The place has been settled for more than 20 years, on government land which has become valuable with the expansion of the city. The houses are of brick, with corrugated metal roofs. There is a rough drainage system for waste water, but the garbage is dumped outside a broken brick enclosure that contains about a hundred single-storey houses.

Kimiyabhai, 60, came from Madhya Pradesh. She lives with her younger, unmarried son, an unskilled labourer on a construction site. Her older son is married, but she is not on speaking terms with her daughter-in-law. Kimiyabhai works as a domestic servant, earning Rs300 a month:

> I weep because I lost my husband, and I wonder what will happen to me when my younger son marries. Will his wife permit him to care for me? Where will I find my food? Where will I sleep? It is hard to be working at my age. I feel giddiness in the morning, my body aches.

Honi, in her sixties, is from Kanpur, and has lived here since she came 20 years ago. She works as a maidservant, cleaning vessels and chopping vegetables. Her three sons live separately from her, and her husband is sick, with fever and stomach problems, and has difficulty breathing. He is 70, and ceased work as a labourer a year ago. Their sons give them no help. Today, Honi has eaten *gobi alu* (spiced potato and cauliflower) and one *chappati* (flat bread). She cannot afford the medicines her husband needs. The only doctor in the slum is a private practitioner. Yesterday she asked her son for money. His response was to come to their hut and beat his father.

Of course, most people do not abandon their elderly. It is not that they love them less, it is that the expectations of the old have been disappointed. The intensity of care, the constancy of a loving presence – these have been disrupted by social and economic changes over which neither young nor old, and indeed neither rich nor poor, have control.

Seasonal rural–urban migration

The irregular but continuous flow of people between city and country is evident in Bangladesh, where seasonal hunger drives thousands of people to find a living in the city. *Monga*, the lean season, is familiar to country people in Bangladesh, who measure their degree of poverty by the number of months each season without food security: that is, confidence that they will have enough to eat.

The measure varies from year to year, but the flow of migrants works as a slow attrition on the areas they come from. Most return when the precarious moment has passed, but some who have found a more secure livelihood in the city may not. Migrants sit on the footpaths of Karwan Bazar in central Dhaka, waiting to be hired for a day's labour.

Twenty years ago, men were the main family migrants. This has changed. Many women and children now accompany them, since they depend upon daily earnings for food. Remittances are too slow to appease immediate hunger. On the city pavements, at railway stations and river-launch terminals, crowds of unemployed people, beggars and displaced countrypeople may be seen. Many of these have had to sell their crops in advance of the harvest, at a rate determined by intermediaries. Some take loans, or *dadori*, from lenders at interest rates as high as 15 per cent a month.

To prevent migration from the *monga*-affected areas, local economies and infrastructures need to be strengthened. Agricultural processing industries and crop diversification are required, but this has been the position for as long as most people can remember, and certainly since before the Liberation War in 1971 and the emergence of Bangladesh as an independent country.

The staging-post to the city

As people switch from subsistence to a market economy, either by migration or by finding themselves locked in the embrace of an industrial society that has stretched out its unloving arms to embrace them, they enter a world where cash transactions predominate. This makes rising income imperative to answer basic needs which they had previously provided for to some degree from their own resources.

The decline of a subsistence economy is not abrupt. It is eroded slowly, by declining productivity, by growing needs that can be answered only by city markets: the need for a watch, a bicycle, a radio, then a television; for fashionable clothing, for shoes, for a more varied diet and a wider experience than is offered by farm and field.

The movement of goods, especially of food, from rural to urban areas, to national and international markets, and the reverse flow, of goods and services from global or national markets to the rural areas, creates imbalances. These are structured into the declining hold of country life, its festivals, customs and celebrations, over the imagination of a new generation.

Globalisation has reshaped the relationship between city and country. City-made goods and processed foods – fabrics, ready-made foods, cooking oil – displace traditional patterns of consumption. I remember standing one wet evening in a shop in Barisal in the south of Bangladesh. Barisal is a city of about 400,000 people, a kind of staging-post for the landless on their way to Chittagong or Dhaka. One of the few occupations in Barisal is cycle-rickshaw driving: ragged, emaciated men struggle across the pot-holed roads, wheels lodged in cracks, sunk in puddles, splashing passers-by with muddy rainwater. The places of greatest animation in the city are the river-launch terminal and the bus-station – exit points on the frontier between country and city. The little store, with its row of electric bulbs threw a bright cone of light into the rainy indigo dusk. Here the better-off young people congregate, for *adda* (sociable conversation) and for shelter from the rain. They drink tea made with Lipton's tea-bags in Styrofoam cups, and eat Pringles or Kit-Kat. Their very demeanour exudes the sense of superiority of those whose money power can command modest luxury objects, which distinguishes them from evictees from the watery landscapes of southern Bangladesh.

5
The spectre of the poor

Ever since the early industrial period, fear of 'the dangerous and perishing classes' has haunted the city and its middle-class occupants. Later, in Britain at least, separation of the poor into the 'rough' and the 'respectable' sought to isolate the upwardly mobile from the rest – the unreformed, the unwashed, the criminal classes. The same anxieties still pervade Western cities. Fear of crime, drugs, robbery and mugging ensure that streets are virtually empty once the rush-hour crowds have gone. Visitors from the South to London or Berlin look at empty streets and say, 'Where are all the people?'

In some cities, the poor have been banished, as in the suburban wastelands of Paris – scenes of rioting in the summer of 2006 by young disaffected people of North African descent – and generally in clearly defined areas where strangers are advised not to go after dark. In the rich world, the poor have become a minority: they pose no electoral threat, although their capacity for disruption – crime, racism, gang fights and drug wars – remains considerable.

The 'improvident' poor

Many nineteenth-century commentators had much to say about the profligacy and idleness of the poor, their addiction to drink and low entertainments, their criminal propensities and tendency to waste their money on immediate comforts rather than saving their scant income for more important purposes. The same argument is heard today, although it is influenced by the altered technological landscapes of the age.

Poor people often have a television set, and sometimes a refrigerator. Private goods penetrate the slums more readily than the necessities of basic nutrition and clean water. There is a battle, as it were, between private and public goods, and the former often win, despite their sometimes injurious effect upon health. And for very good reasons: tobacco companies, for instance, faced with falling sales in the rich world, have actively promoted consumption in the South. The presence of a television is increasingly an emblem of inclusion, not merely in the locality, but in the global culture which also dominates local lives. A refrigerator too becomes a necessity when industrially made foodstuffs must be chilled. Whoever saw global publicity and advertising machines go into action to promote effective sewerage systems, clean water or garbage disposal?

Public goods and services are not subject to the same relentless pressure as objects of consumption. It is very easy to draw conclusions about the inability of poor people to organise their priorities, but that is not the real issue. Organisation and agitation for clean water require an enormous investment of collective energy and strength by people exhausted from excessive hours of labour.

Projecting onto the poor

The city has generated many inquiries into the condition of the urban poor. These reveal a host of associations and assumptions. In most accounts by non-government organisations (NGOs) and donors, the poor are strangely devoid of the human complexity which distinguishes the middle class. They are – despite being in 'families' – strangely sexless. They don't have extra-marital affairs, and there are no lesbians or gay men, although there may be prostitutes. As long as these 'organise' in order to gain recognition of the work they do, they will be included in 'coalitions'. The urban poor do not cheat, or make a living by ripping off others, even though drugs, alcohol, crime and violence are often seen as some of the abstract ills attending the privations they endure. The flaws and failings of daily life are absent. Petty theft, getting something for nothing, selfishness and greed cannot be absent from slum dwellers, but these have no place in proposals and projects submitted to donors. Similarly, evaluations of outcomes must justify the expenditure and effort spent in setting up an organisation or movement, so it is a bland and censored poor who inhabit the unread pages of poorly written reports and accounts of successful campaigns and projects.

For more radical campaigners, the poor are seen as a heroic army of victims fighting against marginalisation. They are always organising, resisting, banding into communities of solidarity for collective action and defence against developers, bureaucrats, politicians and exploiters. The urban poor have become a repository for thwarted radical hopes and dreams of a retreating Left. Many popular movements, sometimes supported by NGOs, think of themselves in an oppositional role, and identify with the urban poor.

Criminal sub-cultures, gangs, people who make a living by fraud or dishonesty, people who explore urban spaces for sexual adventure and experiment, the fly-by-nights and the in-betweens, the vendors of forbidden commodities, the sellers of pirated goods and services, DVDs, perfume, cigarettes, medicines and clothing, the young women – and men – who use sex as a means of self-advancement without becoming prostitutes, have barely a walk-on part in the solemn role attributed to them by those who idealise them, and see their search for basic necessities as filling the entire horizon of experience. Indeed, this is also true of the whole industry of sex tourism, illegal lotteries, gambling, fights between dogs or cocks in the slums, the chain-snatchers and pickpockets, the members of political gangs, the employees of Mafiosi and slumlords, and those who intimidate or beat up recalcitrants for extortioners.

But the competent and clever among the urban poor often have other ways of redressing the great social wrongs of which they are victims, rather than by the pallid organisations and community and capacity-building beloved of many agencies set up to help them. They build their own capacities without outside assistance. One of the ways in which social peace is maintained in the cities of the South is precisely by the extra-curricular activity of slum dwellers: those who stray from the prescribed role of demonstrations, street committees, savings groups and payers of loans to donors given in micro-credit schemes. The impatient, young and restless absent themselves from the efforts of those who undoubtedly achieve improvements in their lives.

It is as hard to know how much economic activity in the slums is illegal as it is to judge the extent of high-class fraud and dishonesty, which keeps many of the rich afloat on a tide of black money and shady deals in property out of which big fortunes are to be made. Opportunities for the urban poor to use their energies, creativity and imagination illegally contribute significantly to social 'stability'. If such avenues were closed, who knows what additional degree of disorder might exist in the slums?

Box 5.1 Aziz and the black brides

Aziz has survived in Dhaka by the exploitation of his own charm. He is 22, and has been a garment worker, cycle-rickshaw driver and hotel-boy. He is married. In fact he has been three times married, and none of his brides knows of the existence of the others.

They have one feature in common. All are 'black': that is, their complexion is dark. This is felt to be a misfortune that will jeopardise their matrimonial chances. Since Aziz is comely, and not afraid to work, he has had no difficulty in relieving three poor families in Dhaka's slums of substantial dowries in return for taking their young women off their hands. He knows the poorest people will go into debt to find the money necessary for marriage. It is given partly in kind – gold ornaments, furniture and household goods, a television or bicycle – and partly in cash.

Aziz has made between 15 and 20,000 taka with each marriage. He rents a room, earns the goodwill of a family in the neighbourhood, and assures them that he is a good and reliable worker. His tells how his parents died in floods and his land was washed away, but he will work to make a successful life for himself and their daughter. None of this is true. He disappears with the money into the tenements, slums and backstreets of the labyrinth of Dhaka. It is a risky strategy: if the families catch up with him, he will be beaten, perhaps to death.

Source: Interview with author.

Box 5.2 The gangland widow

Maria lives in Nova Iguacu: in fact an extension of Rio, but a separate municipality which is also Brazil's seventh biggest conurbation. She is a widow, whose husband was involved in cocaine distribution networks. He was enforcer for a gang, and it was his job to collect money from defaulters.

'I knew and didn't know what he did. I closed my eyes to it, because I had two small children, and as long as he gave me money, it was all right. He was supposed to be a driver for a company executive. The car he drove was so big, it couldn't come anywhere near the place we lived. People admired it, and neighbours knew where the money came from. No one blamed me. They envied me my good luck.

One day he came home, and was different. He was restless and kept moving about. Something in his eyes told me he was guilty. I was disturbed. He wouldn't touch the children. He had been drinking. He never took alcohol or drugs – he knew what it did to people where we lived. When he slept, he left his clothes on the floor. I looked in his pockets, and found a packet with US$10,000. I knew this was his payment for killing someone. He always carried a gun, but he had not used it till that moment.

I was very frightened. I took the children and went to my mother. He came for me, and I couldn't refuse to go back. We never spoke about what he had done, but he knew that I knew.

He was shot one day in the street. It was midday, the market was crowded. Everybody knows who killed him. I know. I was given some money by the gang after he died. I didn't refuse it. My children have had advantages that money could buy. I do not know how it will affect their life. I always taught them to be good. But if they don't find work and a place in society, who knows what they

> will do? Perhaps the taint of bad money follows
> us. I was brought up as a believer. I am afraid,
> whether more of the justice of God or the justice
> of gangs I don't know.'
>
> Source: Interview with author.

The urban apocalypse

Apocalyptic stories of breakdown, dislocation and violence
have been resuscitated from Victorian Britain and exported to
the urban agglomerations in the South. *The Challenge of Slums*
is itself a controlled litany of complaint against neglect, the
disorderly growth of cities and the potential for social disturbance.[1] The early nineteenth-century belief that crime, sin and
intemperance are products of shortcomings in character gave
way to a belief that these things were caused by unclean and
unsanitary living conditions. This paved the way for the reforms
of Victorian Britain. The urban poor were blamed, then exon-
erated, then blamed again; and only when it was discovered that
almost half the recruits to the army in 1884 were unfit was it
realised that social and economic conditions – unemployment,
low pay and sickness – were the cause of poverty, rather than
the moral failings of idleness, drunkenness and shiftlessness.

It is one thing to record the revulsion of outsiders against
the urban poor, but the testimonies of the people themselves,
who love their cities, act as a useful corrective. Thus Niji
Akanni writes of Lagos:

> Just how do you stoke your dreams in the ice cold reali-
> ties of this wonderful city? Ask Lagos parents who
> encourage their malnourished kids to improvise 'foot-
> balls' from empty milk tins, crushed sugar packets and

play all day and everywhere: on grilled balconies, on low-traffic streets, empty plots of land, under road flyovers. The parents know how many African soccer stars' multi-million dollar careers started in similar ways.

Ask also the divorced or widowed middle-aged women who sweat daily running beer parlours, food canteens and provision stores to see their children through schools and colleges. They know that educated children may be their only future insurance in a nation that rapidly pushes its non-earning citizens into the grave. They also know how to smoothen the rough edges of life with a regular 'women's night-out' when they dress up and tour each other's stores/homes to drink beer and talk of the latest fabrics from Madras or Dubai markets.[2]

It is easy to feel apprehensive at overcrowding, squalor and the competitive need to survive. But when we look more closely at how cities maintain a reasonable degree of cohesion, and do not, for the most part, collapse into chaos and disaster, it is clear that the view of cities as agents of breakdown is far from justified. There are great reservoirs of affection, resourcefulness and compassion amongst the poor, which make lives tolerable, when they might otherwise be unbearable. While the poor lack political organisation, they do not, as a whole, lack in the core solidarities of every day, both emotional and social. It is impossible to overestimate the spontaneous generosity and the accumulated wisdom of people who have, amazingly, not been embittered by the troubles and losses they have sustained.

6
Slums

The poor are currently the largest producers of shelter
and builders of cities in the world – in many cases,
women are taking the lead in devising survival strategies that are, effectively, the governance structures of
the developing world, when formal structures have
failed them.[1]

The Challenge of Slums, from which this quote is taken,
reasserts the familiar statistic that 3 billion people live on less
than US$2 a day, while 1.2 billion survive on less than US$1.
These figures are a misleading guide to poverty, since they take
no account of self-provisioning and pooled resources, especially in rural areas. People with enough land to answer their
own needs are not poor, but in a market economy where
everything has to be bought in, US$10 or 20 a day may be
insufficient for sustenance.

Rural areas often supply non-marketed goods, services or
amenities to urban dwellers, who remain very poor in market
terms, but less so when they can count on the free gifts that
contribute to self-reliance, including home-grown food, child
care, and provision of social support at times of suffering and
loss. Migrants to the city bring some of these skills with them:
the ability to construct their houses, solidarities of neighbourhood, small acts of mercy to those who share the overcrowded
places they call home. These may be insignificant in the formal
economic calculus, but they can mean the difference between
survival and failure.

In the cities, despite barter, mutual help, neighbourliness and livelihoods that bestride the urban–rural divide, most people depend for most of their needs upon the market; and purchasing power gives a fair account of the intensity of poverty. In rural areas the best measure of poverty is the number of months in the year when people expect food shortages; in the city, the difference between daily earnings and the amount required for food, housing and water provides a rough guide to the depth of want.

The Challenge of Slums makes the point that not all slum dwellers are poor, and equally, that not all the poor live in slums. Most slums, particularly those long established, comprise a range of buildings: two-or three-storey structures of brick and concrete coexist with flimsy provisional shelters of polythene, wood and bamboo. People who have prospered often stay in the slums because it is convenient for work, or they prefer to remain with the familiar community, or because the cost of relocation is prohibitive.

Enclaves of poor people also exist in middle class areas. Slum pockets stand close to, and provide services for, well-to-do apartment blocks and fortified communities. People live on the pavements all over cities, even in the central or commercial areas, staking their claim to a night's rest in the doorways of offices deserted after dark, on traffic islands, under bridges and flyovers and on the perimeter of airports.

Box 6.1 Kibera – Africa's biggest slum

Kibera, the Mathare Valley and the 110 slum areas hold 60 per cent of the population of Nairobi on 6 per cent of the city land. Kibera has the reputation of being one of the largest slums in the world, disputing that distinction with Dharavi in Mumbai and Orangi in Karachi. One BBC correspondent called it '800,000 people living in a ditch'. The truth is that no one knows precisely how many people live in such places. In theory, according to Geoff Sayer of Oxfam, the nine villages of Kibera have 528,000 residents, according to the 1999 census. The area is squeezed between the city centre and the wealthy suburbs of Karen, Lang'ata and Lavington, reserved in colonial times for European settlement.

Since Kenya's independence in 1963, the migration of landless families, predominantly ethnic Luhya, Luo, Kikuyu, Kamba and Kisiis, have seen the population of Nairobi grow from 350,000 to more than 2 million. A quarter live in Kibera, where most still pay rents to Nubian landlords. Land ownership is uncertain. The landlords lay claim to most of the shanties, and register their holdings with the Chief. But they do not generally hold legal titles. These remain with the government.

Kibera, Mathare and the other slums provide the city's labour reserves. Every morning residents stream out of Kibera to hawk wares on the streets, to labour on industrial estates and building sites, and to clean and cook in middle-class homes. When they return in the evening, others leave to take up their posts as *askaris*, night-watchmen guarding the city's homes and businesses.

Few services are provided in Kibera. The water supply has become the business opportunity of private suppliers, who sell at 2–5 shillings (sh) a can, a price rising to 10 sh when there is a shortage. There is not one state school or government teacher in Kibera. Private schools offer such education as is available – another form of private enterprise, in which the qualifications of the instructors are often a minor consideration. As in all slum areas, medical practitioners are also entrepreneurs, selling basic drugs – oral rehydration therapies, antibiotics and painkillers. Sanitation is absent, and the provision of latrines and sewerage systems inadequate or non-existent.

Crime is common; and for young women there is a constant fear of violence, rape, sexual abuse and sexually-transmitted diseases including HIV/AIDS. This is added to declining access to educational opportunities, and responsibility for looking after younger children, fetching water and fuel for cooking fires. At least one in five of the people of Kibera between 15 and 49 is estimated to be HIV-positive.

Order of a kind is maintained, less by police than by private vigilante groups, who will track down and demand retribution from thieves and robbers for people who can pay.

Kibera is a place from which the state is virtually absent. It has been described as a blank space on the map, an island, a limbo. According to the Washington Consensus, which recommends withdrawal of government from virtually every area of people's lives, it ought to be a paradise.

Source: Geoff Sayer, report to Oxfam GB, 2001 (www.oxfam.org.uk).

Expanding slums

Slums expand for a number of reasons, many of which are linked to 'development'. Rural–urban migration is a major factor, but far from the only one. The high fertility rate of earlier migrants adds pressure from within the city and its slums, and overcrowding worsens. As people live longer –

thanks to the availability of medicinal drugs, especially antibiotics – slum areas are home to a growing population of the
elderly. Most continue to work into old age, since there is no
margin of safety in family incomes to provide for them.

The revulsion inspired by slum areas often leads to the
conclusion that the wretched, makeshift homes themselves
create poverty. The remedy appears obvious – demolish them
and the problem will go away. But it is poverty that creates the
sites of desolation where poor people live, not the environment that creates poverty. People build their own shelters
because they cannot enter the official housing market. Many
bring techniques learned in rural areas, where houses are built
by the occupants out of local materials, including earth, cow-
dung, bamboo, straw and wood. These rural structures need
renewal and repair every year, particularly after the rains.
Urban slums mimic them, but the materials at hand are not the
easily replenished substances of nature. Instead industrial
detritus – polythene, metal, packing cases, sacking – is used.
Many slums advertise industrial products: shelters are made
from boxes stamped Made in Taiwan or Produce of China or
This Side Up, former containers of refrigerators, television sets
or washing-machines. They use sacks which contained
fertiliser or pesticides, or more benignly, sugar or flour, the
packaging of relief foodstuffs from international agencies.
They bear, as it were, the marks of the industrial system which
determines people's destiny, but from which they are excluded.

By the late 1970s, over a million people lived in illegal
settlements in Sao Paulo, Rio, Bogota, Lima, Mexico City,
Manila, Karachi, Bombay, Lagos, Cairo and Bangkok. State
attempts at resettling slum dwellers are common, but these
almost invariably mean relocation to a remote place, far from
the source of livelihood. People avoid being resettled where
possible, since the cost of establishing water connections and
power lines in a new settlement, together with a lack of

employment, makes it an expensive option. Some commute in order to keep their job, although this consumes a great deal of time and a good portion of their daily earnings. (See also Chapter 10.) Many sell the plot they are allocated, or the house they have constructed on it, and move back to insecure city sites, from where they can at least reach their workplace.

Relocation is occasionally inevitable – from hazardous sites, or in the wake of mudslides, floods or fires. Resettlement is often offered as a palliative for evictions of people from land that has become valuable, and which has become required for other purposes, usually commercial or residential development.

Forms of tenure

Security of tenure is one of the most complex and urgent issues of all. Insecurity is the most damaging aspect of city settlements, since this influences all other aspects of life. Insecurity also brings a disagreeable reminder of the circumstances that evicted the landless from rural areas in the first place. Uncertainty of their right to remain impairs people's best use of their skills; their lives are circumscribed by the precariousness of existence, and their menaced rights to be where they are constantly subverts the building of the better life which they sought in the cities.

Home ownership, the major form of security in the developed world, cannot be transferred to the cities of the South. Ownership requires loans and prolonged periods of repayment. It ties people to one place, and suggests a settled way of life, which is impossible for many people in the slums. People must adapt and move on, to take advantage of constantly changing opportunities to make a living. Poverty is, in any case, not static. People move in and out of poverty with changing life circumstances, rising and falling over a lifetime according to the number of dependent people in the family.

Rented housing

Privately rented housing is a major form of housing all over the world, and remains widespread in many rich countries. In Germany and France it is common, while 30 per cent of housing in the UK is rented, from local authorities, housing associations or private landlords.

Private renting was highly exploitative in the early industrial era in Britain, and remains so in many places today. Illegal subdivisions are common: properties are divided into smaller units which are then leased or rented (and sometimes sold) by the legal owners. They are at risk from efforts by planning authorities that decide – sometimes arbitrarily – to enforce aspects of planning which may have been infringed for decades.

A dilapidated block in Sao Paulo is typical. Fallen into appalling ruin, it is occupied by scores of families: The *corticos*, or tenements, which were once single dwellings of the rich, or commercial buildings in the city centre, have been illegally subdivided, and are home to a substantial minority of the poor of Sao Paulo. Rua Tomaz de Lima has broken windows, and a ruinous staircase leading to a solid front door. It is in fact a tenement carved out of the hillside, four storeys deep, part of it underground. A central shaft in the middle of the building is the only source of daylight to the dwellings below ground. A metal roof at the base of the shaft sags with garbage thrown from the floors above, and a narrow courtyard at the bottom is muddy from recent storms.

Many landlords are themselves poor, especially in African cities. They construct a shack on their land and rent it, often to single migrant workers. The ability to do this is particularly valuable to households headed by women, since it saves them from having to find full-time work outside the home when their children are very young.

Squatting

Squatters occupy land or buildings without the consent of the owners. Some settlements have existed for half a century or more, and gained unofficial tolerance. Houses built on squatted land are often traded in the market, although the price is usually affected by the degree of perceived insecurity. Many are also sublet, or sub-sublet, in transaction chains that distance actual occupants from the original squatters.

Most squatters build their own houses on the land they squat on. If it is public land, it will belong to the municipality, or to railway, port or development authorities. If it is on private land, it may belong to landowners waiting for prices to rise, or it may be land of disputed ownership, or farmland standing idle. Over time, many squatters come to an arrangement with the landowners. As cities grow, available land decreases dramatically, and fewer newcomers find a place to stay in areas convenient for work. Most squatting is then in peripheral areas. In many countries, 'squatter invasions' take place: overnight a group of families occupy some unused land, setting up rudimentary shelters. As more people join these pioneers, what is effectively a settlement takes shape, and it may be difficult to dislodge without violence or prolonged and unpredictable court action.

Squatters are the least secure of city dwellers, and also the least well served in terms of infrastructure and water services, sewerage and garbage disposal. These are the settlements that earn cities their reputation for squalor. Where such communities have been long established, governments may provide them with basic services, although people are often proactive in making illegal connections to power supplies. It is common for occupants of squatter settlements to organise in order to defend their right to stay where they are, with or without support from NGOs. The organisation is usually at neighbourhood level, but rarely on a scale to achieve conspicuous city-wide improvements. The Society for Promotion of Area Resource Centres (SPARC) in Mumbai has been working towards developing models of security that can be generalised, not only in the city, but also in the wider world.

Public housing

Publicly built houses for rent are common in the West (even though many have been turned over by local authorities to housing associations or other forms of semi-private management), but in the South such construction has rarely reached the poorer populations for whom they were ostensibly built in the first place. The military, bureaucrats and government servants are usually the main beneficiaries of public housing schemes. When poor people do occupy them, they frequently cannot afford to maintain payments, or they sublet, or sell to more affluent people. Many such schemes deteriorate because of poor maintenance, the effects of weather and the use of inferior construction materials.

The most precarious

Informal rentals may include paying for the most rudimentary space – on the sidewalks of India or Bangladesh, where money must be given to the police for permission to remain. The lives of people on pavements are turned inside out. There is no interior; people must cook, eat, wash, sleep and defecate in full public view. They maintain a functional privacy and dignity by withdrawing their gaze from passers-by, as though this protected them from the often hostile stares of strangers.

Some workers pay for beds in crude lodging houses which may be rented in shifts (similar to the conditions in which Irish migrants to Britain lived in the early nineteenth century, of whom it was said that 'the beds were never cold', so quick was the turnover of their occupants). Many migrant workers live where they work. Drivers sleep in cars parked along the city expressway, garment workers on the benches where they sit all day at the machines they operate. Security guards sleep in boxes at the edge of the compound they watch over, while maidservants live on balconies and in the corridors of the houses where they serve. Bonded workers in the sex industry are held captive in cubicles and cells, where they must service numbers of clients over which they have no control.

Managing slums

In 1989 Jorge Hardoy and David Satterthwaite published a comprehensive survey of urban poverty.[2] It was written before the fall of the Soviet Union: almost 20 years on, its analysis remains, but some of the solutions then offered now seem implausible. Urban poverty has become more acute, and since 1989 it has seemed less and less amenable to remedies from national governments.

The authors identified insecurity in vast swathes of urban settlements as the greatest threat to the poor. These are 'transgressive communities', since the people have been priced out of formal markets, and cannot comply with official standards of construction or of safety and hygiene. The cities of the South are in thrall to foreign models and theories. Many official city maps simply show squatter settlements as blank spaces. Fifty years ago, informal settlements were perceived as transitory. It was assumed they would become unnecessary with 'economic take-off'. But even as economies thrived, slums continued to grow.

Through the 1960s and 1970s slums were described as 'cancers' at the heart of the cities, and were routinely bull-dozed, especially under military and authoritarian regimes. This happened after 1973 in Chile, between 1977 and 1980 in Argentina, and in the Philippines under the Marcos dictatorship. People were evicted and often dumped without resources. Justification for this included 'beautification' of the city, the destruction of what were seen as havens for criminals, health reasons, or developmental schemes such as expansion of the commercial centre or infrastructural projects. City spaces were reallocated and placed at the disposal of wealthier groups.

By the late 1970s governments came to accept the longevity of slums, and opted for segregation over annihilation, confining the poor to a declining proportion of the city area. Some city authorities undertook public housing programmes in the 1960s and 1970s, but the dwellings they built were largely too expensive for the poor.

Some countries provided unused land for the poor, belonging to railways or port authorities. Others agreed to land-sharing: private developers would donate part of the site for low-cost housing, as in Bangkok. In Indonesia and Tanzania governments installed infrastructure for sites where people could build. Maintenance, however, remained a problem: properties quickly deteriorate if unattended. Most housing schemes were 'projects' rather than programmes, and reached a small proportion of the urban poor.

More recently, the remedy has been identified as more effective government, both nationally and locally. This is now the answer of the rich world: transparency, good governance and war on corruption will cure all the evils of urbanisation, even if the growth of cities is a consequence of global forces over which governments have decreasing power. With governments crippled by debt and in thrall to the dictates of the Washington Consensus, dealing with urban poverty is subject to so many constraints that initiatives by governments, international agencies, donors and NGOs cannot keep pace with the rate of slum formation.

When national governments cannot control the land market for housing, or afford infrastructural investment and services, the present world-wide promotion of 'decentralisation' leads to greater responsibilities for local administrations, but without the resources to carry these out successfully. This opens the path to privatisation. If governments and municipalities cannot provide services, the argument goes, then let transnational water, power and communications companies do so. Cost recovery is the slogan of the hour, even though in some cities, a majority of people earn less than enough for the barest sustenance.

There is no effective alternative to intervention, by the instruments of local, national or international governance. It is true that governments, particularly in poor countries, have not provided for poor people or enabled them to help themselves. This is scarcely a persuasive reason for privatisation. After all, it was the consequences of policies of non-intervention in early nineteenth-century Britain that produced conditions which made the public health reforms of the mid-nineteenth-century unavoidable. A return to the ideology of this era in the face of urban populations increasing by 70 million people a year is a policy of despair. All that is known about the ill health and exploitation of slum dwellers was won at great cost to human life. The readiness to discard that knowledge is both incomprehensible and inhumane.

Continuing evictions

The Centre on Housing Rights and Evictions (COHRE) paints a very different picture from the UN/HABITAT *The Challenge of Slums*, which states that mass evictions are no longer policy in most developing countries. In February 2004, COHRE registered a current update of some of the ongoing evictions in the world.[3]

◆ **Kenya**: over 330,000 people were to be forcibly evicted from their homes in the Kibera slums for the construction of a bypass and in a bid to clear areas close to railway and power lines. Residents were offered no resettlement, and with nowhere else to go, were likely to become homeless.

◆ **China**: over 300,000 people had already been forcibly evicted in Beijing in preparation for the 2008 Olympics, and thousands more evictions were expected. Beijing police placed more than 200 people under house arrest in February 2004 before they could petition city leaders about the illegal evictions. More than 40 million rural residents had lost the small pieces of land allocated to them by the government as a result of 'redevelopment' projects since China's economic boom in the 1990s.

◆ **India**: more than 150,000 people were forcibly evicted and 18,000 makeshift dwellings demolished in New Delhi in January 2004. The evictees had been asked to pay 7000 rupees (about US $150) for resettlement, an amount they certainly could not afford. In December 2003, more than 75,000 people living in canal-side settlements in Kolkata were evicted without any notice by heavily armed police and paramilitary forces. In Mumbai in 2004 and early 2005, the government demolished 80,000 dwellings all over the city, but especially in Mankhurd and Kandivili. This coincided with the tsunami which devastated Aceh, Sri Lanka and coastal areas of Tamil Nadu. The human-made destruction produced landscapes eerily reminiscent of the tidal wave: nothing remained but a few broken sticks of furniture, scattered *chappals* [simple sandals], rags, fragments of tin, glass and splinters of wood. Many commentators noted the irony of governments mimicking the brutal force of nature.

◆ **South Africa**: in Johannesburg, more than 4500 people were forcibly evicted from their homes in late 2003 and early 2004 despite constitutional protection against evictions.

◆ **Indonesia:** more than 35,000 people were brutally evicted in Jakarta in late 2003 and early 2004 in a bid to clean up and 'beautify' the city, and thousands more forced evictions were planned by the Jakarta City Administration.

◆ **Ghana:** More than 30,000 people living in the informal settlement of Agbogbloshie in the capital Accra were under threat of being forcibly evicted by the Accra Metropolitan Authority.

◆ **Thailand:** more than 100,000 people were expected to be forcibly evicted in Bangkok because of the local government's plan to 'clean up' and redevelop the city.

Between May and July 2005, police in **Zimbabwe** bulldozed thousands of shanty towns in Harare and other cities across the country, making large numbers of people homeless.[4] The authorities continued a massive demolition campaign, despite international protests, tearing down all illegal houses constructed in Harare, Bulawayo, Mutare, Victoria Falls and elsewhere. Residents of Harare's Mufakose township said the police used flamethrowers to burn homes. A third of Harare's 2 million people were living in wooden, backyard dwellings, many erected more than 15 years previously, as residents had coped with a dramatic housing shortage. President Mugabe said the campaign (of demolitions) would rid the cities of 'havens for illicit and immoral practices', and would make way for a 'more salubrious environment'. The police officer commanding Harare said people should leave the cities and return to the rural areas 'where they belong'.

It is significant that when later in 2005 the city of Mumbai destroyed almost as many homes as had been demolished in the whole of Zimbabwe earlier in the year, this barely rated a mention in the Western press. The demolitions in Zimbabwe were particularly condemned since they were seen as a consequence of misrule, and of the redistribution of former white-owned land to African producers. The demolitions in Zimbabwe targeted political opponents of the regime, those who supported the Movement for Democratic Change. Presumably, the Mumbai authorities did not discriminate in razing the homes of their supporters and opponents alike with majestic impartiality.

Regularisation and upgrading

Where people have constructed their own houses, it is often argued that it is both more effective and humane to assist them by a process of upgrading than by providing alternative accommodation. To achieve this, some basic infrastructure is indispensable. Although state provision has been inadequate or incompetent, the reaction against it which led to the 'free' market being left to make provision has led to little if any improvement. In consequence, there have been many attempts at community self-provisioning. In some cities, for example, waste disposal is community-managed, supported by NGOs.

The regularisation of informal settlements has given stability to many slum communities. Some, however, have contested this relatively simple form of acknowledgement of the rights of squatters. Gita Dewan Verma calls into question the wholesale regularisation of slums, since this institutionalises injustice.[5] She cites India's Draft National Slum Policy, published in 1999, which included large-scale upgrading. She calls upgrading a:

> paradigm on the rebound .... Following so many instances of insensitive relocation, often to barren places on the periphery without livelihood or services, this has been regarded as an acceptable alternative. There is no promise of tenure.

Slum improvement, according to Verma, only exacerbates poverty, and creates a gulf between poor people and those who enjoy decent standards. Second-rate provision for the poor institutionalises inequality. The policy says nothing about preventing slums. The consolidation of shelters on cramped plots has a detrimental impact on the lives of the people. It also entrenches unequal access to land. Between one-third and two-thirds of the urban population live on one-tenth or less of urban land. According to Verma, it is failed promises to allocate land that have led to the inequitable distribution of the present.

India's slum policy advocates 'integration', that is, physical improvements to the slum location, to integrate the settlement in the wider urban area. Yet all slums by definition are demarcated from the neighbourhoods occupied by better-off residents. Slum dwellers must be registered to 'prevent ineligible beneficiaries being included in the programmes for improvement'. More than this, 'participation' by the people in the programme is required, besides community contributions, user charges and even a consolidated service tax. People must pay to collude with the perpetuation of their own inferiority.

Legality and legitimacy

The Challenge of Slums makes the point that legality is less important than legitimacy:

> Secure *de facto* tenure is what matters to [the inhabitants of cities] first and foremost – with or without documents. It is the security from eviction that gives the house its main source of value. Ownership is not necessarily the most important element.[6]

Similarly, the report argues that too little consideration has been given to small providers of rental accommodation (the more so, since there are more renters than squatters in the world). Aid programmes for rental tenure remain neglected and largely unexplored. Perhaps this is because of the bad reputation of 'slum landlords'. Most landlords in the cities of Africa and Asia are householders who let one room or a part of their house, or own perhaps one or two shacks for letting.

Mike Davis identifies 'indeterminacy of land titles as a major source of insecurity for slum dwellers.[7] It is estimated that 85 per cent of urban residents in the developing world occupy property, land or both illegally. Political, business and criminal elites control vast populations by "protecting" informal settlements, as long as these continue to support or bribe them.'

Housing is not becoming more affordable in the world. With higher urban populations, pressure on land, declining employment opportunities, less secure livelihoods and demands by officials for bribes, it is impossible for the poorest to provide themselves with secure accommodation. This has a negative impact upon every aspect of their lives; and indeed, upon the life of the city in general.

7
Livelihoods

Since there are few people to 'give' them work in the slums, poor people show much imagination in providing it for themselves. The distinction is usually made between the 'formal' and 'informal' sectors. The first suggests regular employment, with duly regulated wages and conditions, such as service in government, the bureaucracy and military, financial and banking organisations, the upper reaches of transnational companies, and work by professional and qualified workers. Beneath these are large numbers employed on a semi-formal basis – as factory workers, in retailing, hospitality and transport – while for many (sometimes a majority of workers, the percentage varying from city to city), some form of self-employment in the informal economy is their only source of livelihood. There are also considerable numbers employed in the black or criminal economy.

In most countries of the South, secure and formal employment has been falling in recent years as labour has become increasingly casualised, subject to short-term contracts, or is intermittent and seasonal, and often hazardous and unpredictable. (In India, the percentage of secure formal employment is estimated at less than 8 per cent.[1]) The demarcation between formal and informal is not always clear; and the latter often subsides into part-time self-employment, under-employment and occasional labour, categories that are sometimes separated only by the haziest boundaries.

When I think of the 'informal sector', I remember these people I have met:

◆ a one-legged rickshaw driver in Dhaka, who was injured in the Liberation War, pedalling his vehicle through the tangle of metal on the streets
◆ a street-vending couple in Jakarta who begged me to take their six-month-old son so he would have a better chance in life in my country
◆ dealers who buy the hair of the dead, particularly the lustrous tresses of dead young women
◆ children on the stations of Kolkata filling up discarded bottles of mineral water with contaminated water and re-sealing them for sale
◆ a girl trafficked from Kathmandu to Mumbai by her teacher
◆ a young man whose job is to 'disable' gang rivals in the barrios
◆ intermediaries who rent out portions of the drains in the jewellery quarters of Kolkata and Dhaka, particularly during the wedding season, to labourers who sift through the waste and find microscopic specks of gold
◆ traders in protected species – in Ashok Vihar in Delhi, the bird market does a brisk trade in cockateels, African love-birds, Chinese silky cockerels, African hens, munias, rose-ringed parakeets, rare macaws and finches (a white macaw fetches Rs 180,000, about US$4,000).

Labourers sit at crossings in the cool dawn, their bag of mason's, carpenter's or painter's tools in front of them, waiting to be picked out by potential employers for a day's casual work. Hands are always to be found, to erect tents, arrange chairs and serve food at marriage and birthday parties: raw untutored boys who may get paid half of what is promised, and sometimes nothing at all.

These occupations evoke the survival techniques of nineteenth-century London recorded by Henry Mayhew:[2] the collectors of 'pure' – dog excreta – used in tanning, the mudlarks, children who scavenged the shores of the Thames at low tide, people who spread straw outside the homes of the well-to-do sick and dying to muffle the sounds of the street. In *Our Mutual Friend*, Dickens evoked the grisly livelihood of people who dragged the river in search of the dead. In Bangalore, Mahadev, who is 71, collects the unclaimed bodies of those who die on the footpaths. In 33 years, he has picked up 1500 bodies.

Mike Davis sees 'informal survivalism' as the primary mode of livelihood in a majority of developing-country cities.[3] An informal working class grows side by side with new small-scale entrepreneurs, a disproportionate number of whom are drawn from those made redundant from former state or national companies that have been taken over by international entities. Indeed, the proportion of those employed in the 'informal sector' is a subject for conjecture; like so many of the figures passed to and fro in international conferences and documents published by financial institutions, *no one really knows*. These are arbitrary numbers, the accuracy of which is not regarded as particularly important, since they refer to people of small worth and with no voice.

Davis writes:

> The real macroeconomic trend of informal labour … is the reproduction of absolute poverty. But if the informal proletariat is not the pettiest of petty bourgeoisies, neither is it a 'labour reserve army' of a 'lumpen proletariat' in any obsolete nineteenth century sense. Part of it, to be sure, is a stealth workforce for the formal economy, and

numerous studies have exposed how the subcontracting networks extend deep into the misery of the *colonias* and *chawls*. But at the end of the day, a majority of urban slumdwellers are truly and radically homeless in the contemporary international economy.[4]

The inability of the global economy to absorb this vast displaced humanity creates the potential for an unprecedented disaster. In an earlier age there were 'wildernesses' for them to migrate to. The surplus population of Britain (including felons, the unemployed and the adventurers of the British Empire) was absorbed into 'colonies' throughout the nineteenth century, and the Indonesian resettlements into Kalimantan and Irian Jaya and Brazilian expansion into Amazonia sought to do the same in the twentieth century. But there are no wildernesses left. Indeed, 'settlers' are now almost invariably interlopers, particularly those who take over the land of indigenous peoples, minorities or oppressed peoples, such as Israeli settlers on the West Bank, Bengali settlers among the diluted Chakmas of the Chittagong Hill tracts, and the large-scale population transfers of the Chinese into Tibet.

Box 7.1 Income generation

Many NGOS have made income-generating schemes – especially for women – the focus of their work in slums and rural areas over the past 30 years. The extension of micro-credit to groups excluded from the formal banking system has been a major instrument in this process; and as was discovered by SEWA (the Self Employed Women's Association) in India, the Grameen Bank in Bangladesh, and the hundreds of other organisations they have inspired, the poor, particularly poor women, show a remarkable dependability in repaying what they owe. Since most of these small credit systems are based on groups within particular communities, there is a strong desire (and pressure) not to default.

The honesty of recent rural migrants is also part of the uncelebrated social capital of the slums, as is their neighbourliness and commitment to family solidarity. Poor women are the most reliable borrowers in the world. Of course, conditions on these loans are sometimes restrictive, and occasionally arbitrary. Rates of interest vary: some claim monthly repayments on the whole sum, others take a diminishing rate as the principal is reduced. Proshika in Bangladesh insists it is abusive to take a fixed interest rate as the sum owed declines, and adjusts its rate of interest downwards accordingly.

Source: Jeremy Seabrook, *Freedom Unfinished: Fundamentalism and popular resistance in Bangladesh*, Zed Books, 2002.

'Rag-pickers'

One of the commonest activities in cities is the recycling of waste by what are sometimes called 'rag-pickers', a general term for those who sort through waste, on garbage heaps outside Payatas in Quezon City, in Metro-Manila, the waste mountains of Mexico City and the dumps around Nairobi and Lagos. In some cities, the contribution of waste collectors has been recognised and their work organised. Cooperatives in Peru and Colombia give greater power to the workers in relation to the intermediary or the industrial plant which takes the metal, glass, plastic or paper. But the people are shifting, insecure and not easy to organise. Informal hierarchies of collectors, local go-downs (warehouses), larger warehouses and mass buyers of the waste function with mechanical precision.

In Delhi there are about 200,000 rag-pickers, mainly children and women. They clean up 2000 tonnes of waste each day, saving the city some Rs 1,200,000 (about US$25,000).[5] More than 900 recyclers of waste live under two flyovers in Delhi: they comprise part of the largest informal waste management system in the world.

Chetna, a small NGO in south Delhi, offers child rag-pickers a refuge from the streets, and teaches them how to resist physical and sexual assault. The children are not the wild feral creatures of middle-class imagination. Most are intelligent, their wits sharpened by exclusion.

Box 7.2 The rag-pickers

Azad, aged 8, is a rag-picker. He lived in Gautam Nagar slum before it was demolished in 2000. The people were shifted to Aligaon on the far edge of Delhi. He lives with his uncle and works with an older brother, who provides some protection from violence. Azad gets up at 4.00 a.m. to travel to the city, to sift through garbage before the municipal collectors arrive. He once found a mobile phone, but not knowing what it was, sold it as scrap at Rs7 a kilo.

Ruma, aged 14, lives with five sisters and one brother. Her father is dead and two sisters make a living recycling waste. The family lived in Gautam Nagar until the demolitions. They travel by bus, which costs them Rs10 each way – one-third of their daily income. As the girls move around the city, they risk constant harassment. They are easy prey, young women of no account, used by men accountable to no one. They may be beaten by police, and are sometimes forbidden to get on the buses with their sacks of refuse. Meena, aged 11, checks off on her fingers the amount she gets for each material: Rs5 a kilo for plastic, Rs5 for iron, Rs1 for paper, Rs3 for glass.

Apart from the work of recycling, girls have duties at home. They fetch water, which comes only intermittently, and late at night, to the communal tap. They prepare food. They look after younger children, which involves taking them with them as they work. It is common to see a girl of 12 with a sack over her shoulder and a child on her hip. Occasionally the infants mimic their elder sisters, carrying smaller sacks, so their only experience of play becomes an apprenticeship in the labour to which they are destined.

Aarti's family were dumped in a resettlement area, after their belongings had been trampled and destroyed. Of the resettlement area Aarti says, 'There is nothing there. You cannot work there. Studying is impossible. We only have small oil lamps. All girls do two jobs. Boys keep what they earn, but girls must give to their parents.'

Source: Chetna, personal communication.

The sex industry

The city offers poor young women limited choices. In Bangladesh, most of these are concerned with clothing: they can make clothes as garment workers, they can wash clothes as domestics or they can take their clothes off as sex workers.

Cities, as destinations for male migrants, generate desires that tend to be repressed in rural communities, but which now feed an omnivorous economy. The mobility of truck-drivers, labourers and seasonal workers also creates a demand for sexual services. The city is itself saturated with imagery of sex, wealth and power, the effects of which both disturb and dramatise unmet needs. In most big cities, whole districts are dedicated to sex. For some, this is a major source of revenue from tourists – Bangkok and Manila served as rest and recreation centres for US military personnel, and have maintained this role in their development as destinations for sex tourists.

Whole towns have grown up to service the desires of male travellers. The sex industry, although relatively small, has a disproportionate effect upon the city economy. In India the severe imbalance in the ratio of girls to boys has been exacerbated by techniques of sex-determination before birth, and the abortion of girl children. In the Kolkata sex area of Sonagacchi, however, the reverse was found in September 2004.[6] This area contains several thousand brothels, employing some 9000 sex workers. Here, pregnant sex workers carry a child to its full term only if it is female. Private nursing homes set up in the area perform the 'washing' (that is, abortion) of unwanted male foetuses. In the bylanes of Sonagacchi, girls are conspicuous, including in local schools, which are mostly run by NGOs. The proportion of girls to boys in the schools is 60:40, the reverse of the Indian norm. A girl child is, exceptionally, a good investment. Sex-determination tests, although illegal, cost about Rs500 (US$10). The tenderness shown for a girl child by *masis* or brothel owners is on account of her potential earning power – her virginity is a prized commodity, and much is to be made out of a destiny determined at birth.

The sex industry is inflected by the culture of the country. In Thailand, selling sex is forbidden, but buying it is not. Sex workers are morally judged, but their customers escape censure. The workers offer moral justifications for what they do:

People may think we are stupid, selling our young bodies. We don't think so. It is a struggle to stay alive. We cannot bear to see our parents suffer. They brought us up. They didn't force us into it. And we have no other way of repaying them, because we have no good education and we don't come from rich or influential families who can find decent jobs for us. Our young bodies are all we have to improve the family's economic status. Once we have made up our mind, we have to keep on telling ourselves it is okay to do it. (Young woman from Rim Mon village in the north of Thailand.)[7]

Domestic labour

Domestic labour is the biggest employer of women in the world (as it was in Victorian London). This reflects the growing middle class, and the need of migrant women for shelter with employment. In some countries, girls are sent to work in the homes of the city rich without pay: one less mouth to feed is regarded as sufficient inducement to part with girls of only 7 or 8.

Box 7.3 Jehanara

It was late afternoon when I visited Jehanara's house on the edge of Lucknow. The house is a one-room set, with a small kitchen and bathroom, one of a row built on the margin of a wasting wheatfield. Jehanara's husband was a cycle-rickshaw driver. Early in 2000, he fell sick. A private doctor in the slum where they lived diagnosed diabetes. Since they could neither afford the medicines, nor sacrifice the money he earned, he continued to work. He died in 2002. Jehanara's eldest daughter, Asma, was married at 15. Her other daughters were aged 11, 6 and 3. The loss of income on her husband's death was a catastrophe – only Jehanara's Rs700 a month earned through domestic service remained.

Jehanara arrived home at 4.30 p.m. She is 36, but looks older. She is thin, energetic, with her hair scraped back and dark, mobile eyes. She goes out in the early morning and takes her oldest daughter, who is now 13, to work with her, leaving the two younger at home. This is because she feels, perhaps wrongly, that the oldest, being close to puberty, is more at risk than the youngest two. There is no school nearby and no one to supervise them. When she lived with her husband, they stayed close to her place of work, and she took them all with her. This is now impossible.

Jehanara takes two Tempos (jeep-like taxis, the only form of public transport on the main highway) and then has a walk of 3 kilometres. Her fares eat deeply into the Rs700, and without the generosity of her employers, who give her food and clothing discarded by the girls in their own family, she would find survival difficult.

Jehanara is an emblem of the stolen energies of poor women all over the world, whose desire to look after their own families is disturbed by the superior money power of the family she serves. Such work 'opportunities' impose heavy burdens. The survival of the girls is won at an incalculable cost of abusive damage, inflicted by the unwilling hands of the most loving of mothers.

Source: Oxfam, Lucknow 2004, personal communication.

The garment workers

The garments industry is a major employer of women in the cities of Central and South America, Asia and parts of Africa. Campaigns against conditions in factories that are subcontractors to transnational companies are well known. Naomi Klein details many examples of exploitation by celebrated brand names.[8] Most of these are located in cities of the South, not only in the unvisited sites of overwork in industrial suburbs, but also in the even more secretive free trade zones.

Conditions in the *maquilas* of central America do not deter women migrants to the cities from seeking employment in places which are injurious to health and well-being, and which provide only enough pay for the barest survival. These are not really industrial units; rather, they are places where goods from elsewhere are assembled into garments or other items of basic consumption.

Honduras is now the third largest exporter of garments to the USA, after China and Mexico. There are 176 factories in Honduras which dispatched more than 121 million items in 2002. About 80 per cent of workers are women aged between 18 and 25. Women work minimum shifts, with compulsory overtime. Garment workers suffer serious respiratory problems from inhalation of dust and clothing particles. The atmosphere in the factories and workshops is tense, and bathroom visits are timed. They perform repetitive tasks, at an output rate, characteristically, of two to four pieces a minute. Their daily shift quota may be anything up to 1200 pieces. The basic pay rate in Honduras is about US$100 a month.[9]

Bonuses are forfeited if the workers miss a day, even through illness. The working life of a woman is rarely longer than six or seven years, and the workers change workplace frequently. The women say time spent working in the *maquila* factories is dead years, time taken out of their lives, when they are unable to save. After work, they perform domestic chores, look after children, cook and clean.

Although US companies are the major owners of factories in Honduras, South Korea, Taiwan, Singapore, China and Hong Kong are also significant players. There are no trade unions. Companies are volatile and unstable: in 2001, 34 companies closed down and 30,000 people lost their jobs. Foreign companies can readily open up under another name, thereby evading all responsibilities to pay workers severance pay and benefits. Efforts by women's groups to monitor conditions and ensure minimum standards are undermined by the extreme mobility of garment manufacturers, which can come and go at will, and at a moment's notice. The businesses are almost completely isolated from the local economy. All that remains when they have departed are exhausted workers.

Bangalore is the hi-tech capital of India, its Silicon Valley, boom city and site of jobs outsourced from the USA and UK. It is also a major employer of some 200,000 garment workers. In 2004 I met women garment workers in the office of a support group. Organisation on factory premises leads to direct dismissal, so the closest they can come to a labour union is Cividep, which offers help and legal advice, and a forum for publicising the conditions in which they work.

The pattern in Bangalore reflects cultural circumstances, and most of the 90 per cent female workforce are married. Families migrate from villages after marriage to increase income. Although they do factory work, this does not relieve women of domestic duties. They have greater economic power, which, they point out, is not the same as freedom. Their status may be enhanced, but unmarried garment workers are believed to be of loose morals (similar to seamstresses in Victorian London).

Garment factories are large-scale in Bangalore, employing 2–3000 workers. Five of the six who took part in the discussion worked in the same company. Most were mature women who had been working for ten or 15 years. Most earned between Rs100 and 105 a day (a little over US$2), but one was on Rs73 (US$1.50), less than the minimum wage. The immediate superiors of the workers impose a harsh discipline. When too many qualify for a bonus after working five years, the company closes down and starts up under another name a week later. The workforce is redeployed in the new company, as if they had voluntarily broken their service.

All but one of the women were married. One's husband worked in a liquor shop, one as contract labourer, one as a vendor who had taken a loan for a small shop, another was with the Karnataka Tourist Board, while one husband came home irregularly, and contributed nothing to the household. Since women earn more than their husbands, does this make a difference in men's attitude towards them? The response was ambiguous: 'They respect the money but not those who earn it.'

All the married women had children: some of the children who had left school also worked in the garment factories. Child care is the biggest concern of working women. One woman left her children at her father's house, another dropped them at school before work. All wanted their children to do something better, but work is work, and it is hard for the children of poor people to study.

In the late evening, the women left for home. Their experience is repeated a thousand times in the dark places of the world where cheap clothing for the rich is made. If abuses are exposed in one industrial suburb, the work, which requires minimal infrastructure, wings its way elsewhere overnight, the opportunist bird of passage – and bird of prey – that it is.

The convergence between conditions in garment industries across the globe is astonishing, and identical stories emerge from countries as diverse as Mexico, Indonesia, Bangladesh and Morocco. This suggests that globalisation does have a homogenising influence in the world; and whatever variation there is in 'local' conditions, this does not prevent familiar patterns of exploitation and loss.

Shadow work

No one knows how many people in the cities of the South make a living by the manufacture, distribution and sale of fake goods. Between 5 and 7 per cent of trade world-wide – about US$400 billion – is lost each year to illegal knock-off producers. The US movie industry alone lost US$3.5 billion in 2002. In the same year, sales of illegal CDs were worth US$4.6 billion. Almost half the counterfeit products seized by US Customs came from China, and 27 per cent from Taiwan.

The cities of China and India are major centres for the making and distribution of fake branded goods, pirated merchandise, music and films. Much is for home consumption, and most are small-time operators, models of enterprise, ingenuity and improvisation, working in the interstices of growing cities. It is not that they will not work legally, but legal employment is not available. Their labour is prohibited under rules drawn up by the WTO, particularly those designed to protect patents and trade-related intellectual property rights. Since the cities themselves are counterfeit – the skyscrapers and imposing structures of downtown Shanghai and Mumbai are facades, behind which millions of poor people eke out an existence of bare survival – it is not surprising that fake goods are a major product of these centres of conspicuous but deceptive prosperity.

However that may be, traders in bogus wares are highly visible on the streets of Chengzhou, Shandong and Kolkata: selling perfume the colour of urine in plastic flagons, watches encrusted with false jewels, branded fashion wear, handbags, accessories and jewellery from the most celebrated ateliers of Europe and North America – all available at knockdown prices from makeshift stalls. Films not yet released by Bollywood, CDs which have yet to leave the legitimate factories, the designs of tomorrow, or even the day after, make a premature appearance on the streets. Salespeople, alert and vigilant, are always ready to pack up and disappear into the dark alleys between the main roads if there is a raid on their illegal activities.

The producers of such goods might, in other circumstances, have been traditional artisans. Instead they are victims of the fall in demand for ancient crafts and skills, whose sustainable and renewable artifacts have been usurped by mass-produced goods. The sly subversion of global consumerism may be read as the revenge of the marginalised and those degraded by the global market. The growing profession of fakers recruits from the increasing army of the underemployed and disemployed.

One of the unanswered questions thrown up by the slums is this: on what moral basis does a global economy, much of which is devoted to the cultivation of appearances, images and symbols, a world of inauthenticity and illusion, complain of fakes, rip-offs and forgeries? When the injured and humiliated of the subcontracted dungeons of global brand names are used up in the production of football shirts or trainers, locked into factories at night, watched by CCTV when they visit the lavatory, beaten or raped by overseers, who will grieve over the dented profits of merchants of global deception? When counterfeiters and institutionalised purveyors of falsehood rule the world, their imitators, struggling at the limit of material survival, represent a subversive reality which they can scarcely be expected to understand.

Rakesh has been working with Sarai in the labour market of Lajpatrai near the Red Fort of Delhi, an elaborate network which makes and distributes fake CD players, DVD players, television sets, sound systems and other electronic equipment.[10] Rakesh described the conditions of work to me.

> People work for unlimited hours, unorganised, produc-ing entertainment equipment they cannot afford for themselves. There is a labour force of about 3500 people, all migrants from Bihar and eastern Uttar Pradesh. In addition to the assembly workers, there are around 500 engaged in packaging and 2000 *thelawalas* and *jhalliwalas*, who transport goods by trolley or bamboo basket. They are exploited by employers, shop-keepers, the municipality and the police extorting bribes. They work at piece rates, getting Rs5–10 per item, which takes about an hour to make.
>
> Unlike the workers, the shopkeepers are well organ-ised and have links to government departments, so they are at no risk of disruption. The faking of 'intellectual property' is a different industry, and under greater pres-sure from entertainment corporations, film makers and musicians. This is why there are many raids on the soft-ware industry, and far fewer on this version of manu-facturing, much of it out of cannibalised and second-hand components. It is not subversive, but rather mildly transgressive, for it provides access to many people who would otherwise be excluded from the market.

8
Cities of fear

The partition, segmentation and division of cities leads to increasing separation of the rich from the poor. The growing lack of contact between the two leads to fantasy and paranoia, but also to a form of economic apartheid. The rich, seeking security in gated communities and policed enclaves of privilege, see the poor as agents of social disintegration and breakdown. This sometimes becomes a self-fulfilling prophecy, since desperation may indeed generate violence and crime. Although criminal gangs, kidnappers, drug mafias and people traffickers constitute only a small minority, these feed a discernible sense of urban paranoia.

In 2002 there was extensive violence in Godhra in the Indian state of Gujarat, involving fatal attacks on the Muslim minority in the state by mobs of Hindus. In Ahmedabad meanwhile, in the city centre people were tranquilly visiting cinemas and restaurants, as though the carnage had nothing to do with them. While certain slum areas in Central and South America are dominated by drug lords, and have become off-limits to official governance, planeloads of privileged inhabitants take off from their airports, for medical treatment, shopping or vacations in North America. In Naples, Italy in December 2004, a conflict between groups controlling the drugs trade turned the desolate suburb of Scampia into a battleground, where 28 people were killed in a month. Metal gates and grilles have been installed in the walkways and stairs of some blocks of flats. The *Camorra* gangs have placed them there, so that they can be locked by drug dealers as they flee the police.[1]

Crime

In October 2004, police shot dead a drug dealer known as Gangan in the Rio de Janeiro *favela* of Sao Carlos. He had been a high-ranking member of a well-known cartel. The authorities blocked all exits and entrances to the hillside *favela*, in order to forestall any backlash, since residents and gang members often riot when their patrons are killed.[2]

Many drug lords are benefactors to slums, providing forms of social security which neither the state nor the formal market supplies. Observers report that killing senior members of drug-gangs may exacerbate violence, since the power vacuum leads to struggles for succession and efforts by rival gangs vying for power. Some gangs run semi-charitable enterprises in the slums, paying for health care, education and even providing food to those who support them. In certain cities, particularly where state institutions have receded or reduced their intervention, social governance has in fact passed to other actors, often with a political-criminal connection. This is a pathological version of the 'privatisations' which are, in other circumstances, recommended by global financial powers.

The cities of South Africa live with structures set up at the time of apartheid, which still deeply influence the patterns of crime. Cities were characterised by diffuse low-density construction, and fragmentation and separation by land use, income group and race. Most employment was in the centre, while residential areas lay on the far periphery. The unequal city structure has lent itself to continuing separation, characterised this time not by race, but by economic status. This lends itself readily to opportunistic crime, especially since the poor have to travel farthest to reach places of work, with numerous changes of trains, buses and taxis.

The long distances travelled leave some peripheral communities virtually deserted for many hours, while most inner-city areas become ghost towns after dark. Residual central residential zones lose their attraction and fall into decay. The open spaces between settlements cannot be adequately policed, while public areas between dwellings are the responsibility of no one. Segregation in South African cities has been more dramatic and intense than in most other countries, but they exhibit similar developments which provide abundant scope for crime.

This is not merely a technical matter: the legacy of apartheid, expressed now in the great gulf between rich and poor, is a structural problem, and one which affects most cities in varying degrees. The reaction to crime itself influences the cities. Suburban houses are increasingly fortified, with fewer outer windows, while suburbs are surrounded by fencing, barriers and have limited access. Crime creates greater social distances between rich and poor, and this is made easier by the spatial divisions inherited from the apartheid era.[3]

Rory Carroll, writing of the growth of fortified cities in South Africa in 2005, reports:

> The concept is medieval but the execution is very much 21st century: a fortified town run as a miniature state. Rising from the winelands outside Cape Town, Heritage Park is enclosed by a computer-monitored fence that zaps intruders with 35,000 volts and alerts a corps of security guards. The newly built cluster of 650 houses, two churches, two schools and several factories on the outskirts of Somerset West could claim to be the safest town in crime-plagued South Africa.[4]

Caroline Moser states that 'urban crime and violence prevention and reduction is now a growth industry.'[5] In other words, increasing inequality (a more reliable indicator of urban violence than poverty) engenders new forms of insecurity, which are then transformed into further opportunities for economic growth. Indeed, crime becomes not so much a matter of security as somebody else's business opportunity. This is, perhaps, what happens when economic growth becomes the supreme goal of society: what is supposed to be the universal panacea for exclusion, and indeed all other social ills, turns out to be a fearful generator of new forms of poverty, and novel kinds of violence.

Which are the most violent cities has been the subject of much debate. It is usually judged by the homicide rate per 100,000 inhabitants; but published figures are unreliable. Bodies never found, killings in slums where the police do not go, institutionalised cultural violence against women and children – 'honour' killings, dowry deaths disguised as accidents, contrived road 'accidents' that get rid of rivals – there are good reasons to question official figures. Among cities high in official tables of global insecurity are Johannesburg, Rio de Janeiro, Washington D.C., Bogota, Medellin, Sao Paulo, Detroit, Moscow, Manila, Addis Ababa, Gaborone, Kingston, Caracas and Lagos.[6] To these may be added Baghdad and Mogadishu.

Crime and fear of crime immobilise millions of city dwellers. With a homicide rate of 23 per 100,000 people, Brazil is one of the most violent countries in the world. There were 44,000 killings in 2003 – the equivalent of a medium-sized war, and over 1000 times more than the number of US soldiers killed in Iraq between March 2003 and the end of 2004.[7] Sao Paulo is one of the least safe cities. Even those who regard the private vehicle as a secure means of transit sometimes find themselves robbed by thieves at gun-point in traffic jams. The children of prominent families are regularly accompanied by bodyguards as a precaution against kidnapping: Rich businesspeople and their children are the usual victims.

Fire in the cities

Fear comes in other guises. Rasna Warah writes:

> Shortly after dark one night, a Molotov cocktail descended on a squatter community on the northeastern outskirts of Nairobi, Kenya's capital city. Fortunately, the 2000 or so residents were not asleep and no lives were lost. But they lost everything they owned, including beds, stools, clothes, crockery. The fire was no accident. Like many arson attacks on informal settlements in the country, it was meant as a warning – leave or die.[8]

The use of arson to clear slums is well documented in most major cities; but accidents, too, are equally common, from faulty electrical installations, illegal connections and spilt kerosene. Disastrous fires have devastated communities in Bangkok, Mumbai, Manila, Jakarta and Mexico City.

Box 8.1 Fire in Dhaka

In November 2004, fire destroyed a market in Dhaka, Bangladesh, gutting about 1800 shops in the Gulistan area. One person was killed and 15 injured. The market, owned by Dhaka City Corporation, houses small, often rudimentary shops and booths, selling clothes, bangles, shoes, leather and plastic goods.

This was one of the less damaging fires in Dhaka in recent years. On 3 May 2004, nine women were trampled to death and 50 others injured when they ran for their lives after a false fire alarm at a building housing several garment factories in Dhaka, which together employ between 4000–5000 workers.

In 2001, 24 workers were killed in a fire at the Mico Sweater Factory. In 2000, 48 workers were killed in a fire at the Choudhury Knitwear Factory.

Between 2000 and 2004, 132 slums were gutted in Dhaka, razing over 24,000 shanties, and making more than 150,000 people homeless.

Source: www.cleanclothes.org.

More than 70 major fires have occurred in Bangkok in the past three decades. In 2001, within two days, fires in Phnom Penh made more than 20,000 homeless. In December 2004, 1000 people were made homeless when the Nargis Dutt slum in Bandra was gutted in less than an hour. The people had only just been evicted from the Bandra–Worli sealink, so that a promenade could be constructed. Delhi has more slum fires than any other city in India.[9]

Violence against women

Violence against women in slum areas is exacerbated by social and economic changes. The withdrawal of government services means that greater burdens than ever are placed upon women, since they must increasingly enter the workforce without relinquishing any of their responsibility in taking care of the family, fetching (sometimes buying) water, cooking and cleaning. As a direct result of these added burdens, tension in poor households rises, and women are blamed by men for developments that are beyond their control. In many cities, including Dhaka, violence is a male reaction to women's advancing social and economic emancipation.

Violence against women is also a response to the growing sexualisation of society, which is in part a consequence of consumerism. Attacking and mutilating women with acid is now a feature of Bangladesh: men who are spurned by women with whom they are infatuated have used this as a form of revenge. There have been, on average 33 attacks a month since January 2000. In Dhaka alone, there were 246 incidents with 327 victims. Acid throwing has also been attributed to unmet dowry demands, family feuds and land disputes.[10]

Despite campaigns against dowry in India, the proliferation of consumer goods has increased pressure on families to provide brides, not only with traditional wedding jewellery, but also with a growing range of goods. A bicycle, a television set, a refrigerator, a motorbike, a washing machine, a three-piece suite, as well as large sums of cash, are now routinely expected.

Box 8.2 Jagdish and Gurubai

Jagdish and Gurubai are pious conservative Hindus. In the principal room in their home in Delhi are a large wooden bed, a television, a music cassette player, and a telephone on a chest of drawers, where garments are stored. On the wall, garlanded with fresh marigolds, is an enlarged studio portrait of a young woman, their daughter, smilingly unaware of her fate. She was married in 1999 to a man from Meerut in Uttar Pradesh. The family provided her with a dowry of Rs50,000 and some household goods. After two years, her in-laws began to place pressure on her, and hence on her family, to increase the dowry, which all parties had agreed to at the time of the marriage. Such events often follow the internal collapse of the marriage relationship: antipathy, non-consummation, of the resentment of a mother-in-law.

Jagdish and Gurubai could not meet the demands. The animosity to the young woman culminated in an attack upon her in her kitchen. She was doused in kerosene and set alight. Badly burned, she was brought to Safdarjang Hospital in Delhi. She survived for 27 days before succumbing to burns. The father-in-law was prosecuted and received a prison sentence of ten years.

Source: personal communication.

The police and the military

Stories like Jagdish and Gurubai's suggest that poor people, especially women, are at risk from violence inside, as well as outside, their families. In many countries, extra-judicial killings by police and military forces take a disproportionate toll of the poor. In Brazil, where slums represent a parallel world to that in which the middle class live, the police enter only for military-style raids. In 2003, almost 1000 people in Rio state were killed in confrontations with the police. In Thailand, between 2002 and 2003, hundreds of people died in a 'crackdown' on drugs. Many were killed by police, although the government presented their deaths as a consequence of 'feuds' between rival gangs. In Bangladesh there were hundreds of extra-judicial killings in 2004; many of the victims were described laconically as 'killed in crossfire'. Most were shot by members of the Rapid Action Brigade, an elite government force, which was deployed in 2004 to response to a deterioration in social order. Those killed were almost invariably described as militants, extremists or members of 'underground parties'. In Colombia, in the 25 years to 2003, 102 people were killed as a result of political violence, and between 50,000 and 200,000 people have died in battles between the government, Leftist groups and right-wing militias, which were formed to protect landowners from Leftist guerrillas.[11]

The houseless mind

Crime and fear of violence add new forms of insecurity to all the familiar vulnerabilities. The uncertainties of rural life are known, but the city presents new forms of unpredictability and dislocation. These create widespread psychic disturbance. In the early industrial era in Britain, the extent of mental disorientation may be read in the fact that in the 1780s there were about 40 lunatic asylums in England and Wales; by the 1840s, there were over 400.

There are no official figures for the incidence of breakdown and psychiatric illness in most cities: this is no more a priority for impoverished city governments than is improving the conditions in which prisoners are held in jail. In India, official estimates of the mentally ill – between 10 and 20 million – understate the problem.[12] There are a number of reasons. Continuing networks of support still contain all but the worst afflicted. This may lead to shame and concealment, but the sick person will be protected by his or her family and neighbourhood. One consequence is that only the most visible cases come to the notice of the authorities, and these people are as likely to be jailed for 'criminal' offences as to receive treatment.

There is also a high level of tolerance of 'strange' behaviour on the streets: there is enough ragged misery and want to justify the most bizarre conduct. The city streets are full of 'invisibles', unkempt unbathed men, occupying doorways and cardboard cartons, singing or talking to the voices in their head; the messiahs and the outcasts, the derelict and the broken. Only violence draws attention. Lone women with mental health problems also roam the streets, but since these are in greater danger of being molested, they are more likely to be removed.

People who work with the psychiatric casualties of urbanism have one of the most thankless tasks. They rarely have donors to impress with targets met and achievements accomplished. Dr Joyce Sirimoni in Kolkata is now in her 70s. She has worked with sick women for 40 years, providing accommodation for those released from asylums. She began in Bangalore, where the only premises she could find were a disused burial ground; a fitting site for the living dead. 'They are indeed dead to their family, to society and to the world,' she comments.[13] Alcohol and drug abusers were her first patients, but suicide prevention soon became a priority: suicide remained a crime until the 1970s, and the police – ever watchful for a source of extra income – extorted money from those who had tried, unsuccessfully, to take their own lives.

Joyce Sirimoni visited the 800 'non-criminal lunatics' in one of Kolkata's asylums early 1990:

> It was a shocking sight. Three huge cells with padlocks and barred gates. Some women were naked, the ward was filthy, there were no separate toilets. At the time of giving food, the ayahs went with sticks to beat those who would fight for a bigger share. Women were crying out 'Ami pagal noi,' I am not mad. Many had been locked away by their families, because they were an embarrassment. One woman tending the patients with great care was serving a sentence for murder. She was gentle and affectionate. I took her to help in the rehabilitation center I planned. She had been a cabaret dancer, but she was one of the best nurses I ever saw.[14]

The sanctuary now run by Dr Sirimoni is a building which had been lying derelict for 25 years. The roof leaked, birds had made their home in the structure, shrubs grew out of the masonry. Within three months, it was repaired and a six-bed unit established. 'With so many people evicted from homes and livelihoods, why should we be surprised at people also driven out of their mind?' Most women are eventually reintegrated into the community, and find some livelihood – making papads (crisp breads), weaving, tailoring, block-printing, or making *agarbatti* (incense sticks).

It is also reported that frantic lifestyles, peer pressure, career demands and unlimited wants are causing stress, anxiety and depression among teenagers. Twenty-five per cent of patients consulting psychiatrists in Delhi are children. Delhi now sees between 2500 and 3000 cases of heart patients below 13 years of age each year. Poverty drove one Dalit student to suicide. His father, a labourer on other people's fields, said the boy, 17, needed Rs275 for computer fees. There is a daily toll of suicides, usually by hanging from a ceiling fan – brutalised brides, deserted women, unhappy students, indebted labourers.[15]

This toll of humanity is usually described in a brief paragraph in newspapers. A 22-year-old man drowns himself in a tank in Bangalore after his parents arranged his marriage. Police suspect Anand was upset because he was not interested in getting married. A 16-year-old girl commits suicide in Delhi 'because she was upset over her exams'. In Delhi, a survey by the Institute of Human Behaviour and Allied Sciences found that about 11 per cent of the people in the capital had thought of committing suicide.[16]

A girl in Delhi was raped by the principal and vice-principal of a college, who promised her good grades if she keeps silent. Pavement dwellers are killed as they sleep by a drunken driver. A building collapses. A man buys a woman to bear him a child when his wife turns out to be infertile. A kidney is taken by stealth for sale by a surgeon who is operating on a woman for some minor disorder. Schoolchildren die through the incomplete cooking of manioc. Infants are traded to childless western couples. Glimpses of stories of unimaginable dispossession only hint at the underside of global 'development' in which only the success stories are given space in the mainstream global media.

9
Provision of basic services

Insecurity is almost always accompanied by inadequate services. Of the poorest 20 per cent of urban dwellers in the developing world (sub-Saharan Africa, North Africa and the Middle East, Asia and the Pacific, Latin America and the Caribbean), 40.6 per cent have water connections, 9.7 per cent have sewerage, 61.6 per cent electricity, 17.4 per cent telephone connections (although the advent of mobile phones makes this figure less relevant) and 71.2 per cent access to water. For the richest 20 per cent the figure is well over 90 per cent, except for telephones (87.6 per cent).[1]

In towns and cities across Africa, service provision, never comprehensive, has faltered dramatically. The total percentage of those with piped or well water on the premises is 41 per cent, with less than 30 per cent of the urban poor provided for. In the total urban area, 21.7 per cent of people have a flush toilet and 66.8 per cent a pit toilet. The figures for the urban poor are 13 per cent and 65.9 per cent respectively. Electricity reaches 41.5 per cent of the urban population, but only 19.7 per cent of the urban poor. Almost 63 per cent of the urban poor lack these three basic services.[2]

Small private operators are suppliers of water to many urban households, which makes safe drinking water even more expensive to the poorest. Sewerage systems are either broken down or non-functioning in many areas, and do not reach new slum areas. Some community organisations have provided their own, following the most well-known of all, the Orangi system in

Karachi. It is a tribute to the poorest that in spite of relentless workloads, they still manage to work creatively together for the collective good in many places; although it means even greater burdens upon those who are not only the most exploited if they are to gain access to amenities which the rich take for granted.

Solid waste services reach less than one-third of the people of urban sub-Saharan Africa. Electricity exists in most city slums, but much provision is through illegal connections. These are dangerous, and sometimes lead to spectacular fires. In the flooding of Mumbai in the 2005 monsoon, when almost a metre of rain fell on the city, many of the several hundred fatalities were caused by electrocution, faulty wiring and dangerous connections exacerbated by the rain.[3]

Roads in poor areas of developing countries are poorly maintained. Some slums are inaccessible to vehicles. Roadways subside and collapse, or are pitted with holes, which makes the approach to informal settlements difficult and risky. Damage from rain and floods is repaired patchily, if at all.

Some police are corrupt. Like some government employees, they regard the poor as a means of augmenting a low salary. They sometimes form alliances with the criminals they are supposed to pursue, and many slum dwellers are squeezed between criminal gangs and the ostensible keepers of law and order. The rise of local vigilantes, informal enforcers of the order of slum lords and Mafiosi, is matched in many places by a rough-and-ready welfare system provided to the slum people by criminal networks, which have displaced official agencies of provision. This earns them the allegiance of deprived populations, and places people at an even greater remove from official agencies of the state.

While about 80 per cent of children attend primary school, this falls to 57 per cent of those between the age of 15 and 16.[4] More boys than girls attend school. Millions of children work, and their contribution is vital to family survival. 'Child labour', which appals many observers, does not appear in the same light to children accustomed to learn through work, on family land, or to children in small restaurants, working in small-scale transport, domestic labour, repair workshops and markets. When adults cannot procure a secure sustenance for their family however hard they work, it is inevitable that children, and indeed the elderly, should continue to contribute to the limits of their power.

Campaigns against child labour are one thing, but until adults receive wages that enable them to answer the needs of their families, the work of children will continue to be vital. It is perhaps less glamorous to fight for fair wages for adults than to evict vulnerable and abused children from the workforce, but who is going to espouse the cause of the impoverished members of informal adult workforces? It is both their function and their destiny to provide the casual, intermittent and insecure labour which fuels the well-being of the beneficiaries of city growth, the professional and well-to-do communities.

Education and health services

The failings of government schools include shortages of almost everything: dilapidated desks in overcrowded and ruinous buildings, teachers who fail to turn up, or who set the children chanting by rote, and then fall asleep at their desks. Government cuts in provision and corruption in municipal authorities open the way for privatisations which are beyond scrutiny, especially in poor areas. Schools with names like Little Flower, Happy Garden or Bluebell are run by semi-literate entrepreneurs. The best schools are equal to any in the world, but these dumping grounds for the children of the poor ensure social apartheid and perpetual inequality.

In any case, education often means preparing children for a world which does not exist; or if it does, it remains out of reach of the great majority. Education often destroys their capacity to labour in traditional occupations, without offering them entry into the secure livelihood and the better life which is the essential promise of education. One of the most striking contrasts in African cities is between the eagerness of young people to learn in dilapidated and ill-equipped schools, and the cynicism and brutality of the real world which they will finally enter. In the cities young men with qualifications in business administration take their precious 'biodata' from one unwilling employer to another, and grow impatient with what they see as the broken promises of learning. They become a rich recruiting ground for criminals, and ultimately, if there is no place for them in the city economy, even terrorists.

Health care and social services are also haphazard, and absent from many slums. There is a proliferation of private doctors in the slums – some of them with doubtful or fraudulent qualifications. People readily use traditional healers, and herbal and folk remedies for sickness. A combination of worsening physical conditions in the slums and the loss of state-provided health care leads to a deterioration in the health of the people, even when mortality decreases. (In many countries of Africa, of course, HIV/AIDS has lowered life expectancy.) Although child mortality in the urban areas is lower than in the rural hinterland, it is nevertheless higher among the urban poor than in other parts of the city. This is why generalisations about 'the city' and city-wide statistics are misleading: they combine figures relating to the very rich and very poor.

Social security networks

The family remains in many cases the most significant provider of care, although, as was noted earlier, migration and poverty tend to disrupt family support networks, and they cannot be relied upon in all circumstances. Girls, some of them very young, take responsibility for their younger siblings, while the infirm elderly are a growing burden. Rising life expectancy has been largely due to the ready availability of a few basic drugs, particularly antibiotics, and the accessibility of oral rehydration therapy for children with diarrhoea and other waterborne diseases.

The survival of the elderly is a mixed blessing. As long as they look after children, take care of the house when other adults are working, prepare food or work at home, selling some small commodity on the threshold of the hut – making paper bags, cooking and selling snacks – they are an useful resource to the family. But when they are sick and infirm, they fall into the brutally expendable category of yet another mouth to feed.

The decline in purchasing power caused by the imposition of 'cost recovery' schemes in health and water supplies, and the removal of subsidies under structural adjustment programmes, have placed new strains on the urban poor. AIDS orphans, lack of work opportunities for the young, the emergence of street gangs, crime and drugs create additional problems. The number of street children in Zambia doubled to 70,000 between 1991 and 1994, while the number in Nairobi rose from 4500 to 30,000 in the same period.[5] By 2000 there were 60,000.

In spite of this, the commitments of family and wider ties of kinship can show great resilience. Traditional values can be a force for stability, even when they are patriarchal and conservative in nature. Community-based groups, together with support from NGOs, have strengthened resistance to evictions or have secured rights, while the power of religion to sustain people in times of turbulence and dislocation cannot be overestimated. Sometimes religious bodies topple over into destructive cults, like the Lord's Resistance Army in Uganda. They may become a focus for uprising or rebellion against the government, or echo the symptoms of ethnic and religious divisions, as in some cities of Nigeria.

Box 9.1 The hope of the poor

Asha Likele is an example of the positive power of both religion and humanity in the presence of the AIDS crisis. In her early sixties, she lives in Luis Mbeza, on the edge of Dar es Salaam. She looks after six children orphaned by AIDS – four boys and two girls, aged between 5 and 16. These are the children of six dead parents. Originally her elder brother had taken them into his home, but when he too died, she assumed responsibility for all six:

> Allah did not bless me with children of my own. They call me Mother, since all but the oldest came to me very young. Other children tell them I am not their mother, but although they know it, they choose not to believe it.
>
> I live from farming, so the income is small. Ten acres inherited from my father is enough to feed the seven of us and to sell something in the market as well. I rent out a room in my house. One sister helps me work on the farm. Saleh, my eldest, does not want to do farm work. Young people know only money, and think the produce of the earth is worthless because there is nothing to show for many months.

Asha wakes at 5 a.m. and, after prayers, cooks breakfast. In the busy season, she prepares food for the whole day, and works from early morning till 9 p.m., tending, weeding, harvesting her crop of maize and rice. At bedtime, Asha tells the children stories. She tells of a grandfather who had two wives and brought up two families. One was loved and the other was not. The children of the unloved family went to another woman who cared for them tenderly. This is their favourite story.

She teaches the children a humane and tolerant Islam: to love others, respect elders, lead honest lives, and not 'to run here and there' – a euphemism for promiscuity. 'I am sorry for the young people. They have temptations unknown to us – alcohol, drugs, bhang.'

The catastrophe of AIDS is mitigated, not by promises of a phantom 'international community', but by the courage and tenacity of millions of older women, who have become carers of the terminally sick, from whom a global market capriciously withholds basic drugs in the name of freedoms they do not understand.

Source: Jeremy Seabrook, *A World Growing Old*, Pluto Press, London, 2003.

Urban waste – rural regeneration

The growth of cities is sometimes represented as a blight on the surrounding rural area. It does not have to be. Not only is a large proportion of urban waste collected and recycled by poor women and children, but urban wastes may be rich in nutrients for crops, although a failure to sort dangerous materials from organic matter means that indiscriminate use of wastes on agricultural fields may do more harm than good. If the organic material is isolated, it can make cultivation possible on even the most degraded soils.

Bamako in Mali and Ouagadougou in Burkina Faso have both grown rapidly.[6] Neither has the resources to collect and dispose of urban wastes – 600–700 tonnes a day in a city of a million people. The organic portion of this amounts to about one-third; but plastic, metals, textiles, chemicals and other noxious substances need to be separated if organic matter is to be safely recycled.

After independence, municipal authorities assumed responsibility for collecting waste. By the 1990s, expanding cities and declining income led governments to turn to waste-management enterprises and non-profit organisations, some supported by NGOs, to assume responsibility for basic services. Small enterprises, some depending on donkey-carts, carry waste to depots in the neighbourhood and sort out valuable components, while municipal trucks dispose of the rest.

Farmers around Ouagadougou grow staples of millet, sorghum and *niebe* (or cowpeas, a local legume), and keep some livestock. The Niger River in Bamako offers opportunities for more diverse cropping. Most farmers in the wider urban area along the river cultivate vegetables and fruit as well as sorghum, millet, rice and peanuts, including garden peas, tomatoes, onions, okra and strawberries.

The agricultural land around Bamako is farmed by local residents, who have customary tenure rights. These have been joined by retired civil servants from the city, who purchased land concessions as a form of pension. Both classes of farmer grow staples for home consumption and fruit and vegetables commercially, for which demand from the city is increasing.

Farmers themselves usually sort out the larger inorganic objects from waste, and spread the remainder on their fields before the rains start. This has enabled previously unused land to be brought under cultivation, and has restored fertility to degraded soils. However, semi-decomposed waste is a hazard, both to farmers and to consumers of the food they produce. Dangerous pathogens may be present, and there is constant risk of contamination from plastic bags, glass and batteries, which produce lead and cadmium that pollute soil or water tables. Farmers are willing to pay for urban waste. In Bamako, they pay €2.90 a tonne for sorted solid waste, but some unsorted waste inevitably finds its way through unauthorised routes to the fields.

Urban waste should be seen, not as a dangerous and unwanted nuisance, but as a resource full of nutrients for agriculture. The process of collection and sorting can only be accomplished at neighbourhood level to establish close collaboration between the processors of waste and the farmers: the promotion of inter-dependent livelihoods will advantage collectors, processors, distributors and users of the organic waste that remains. It is an obvious area for small-scale enterprise, since neither municipal authorities nor big private entities are going to be successful.

Water

The lack of provision of sewerage systems, garbage collection, drainage systems, power connections and passable roads to the communities of the urban poor are all well documented. Here, we shall look at the element least dispensable to human survival – water. The prospects for the urban poor must be viewed in the light of a decline in municipal or state supply and the increasing replacement of these notoriously inefficient suppliers by commercial markets.

Local governments cannot possibly maintain supplies to rising city populations. Whether the most creative way of facing this reality is to withdraw public investment is another question. The advocates of this course of action assume that private providers will fill the gap: evidence of the continuing faith-based confidence in the magic of markets.

Ivan Illich charted the way in which water, the source of life, an object of worship, mystery, purification and cleansing, was transformed by industrial society into the formulaic commodity H_2O.[7] This continuing process has now reduced what is indispensable for life to a product to be purchased – another step in the marketing of life itself.

Much energy has been expended by investors, brokers and dealers in commodities to make this process more acceptable. One method has been 'user participation'. This means the establishment of a two-tier system of water provision, whereby those who can afford to pay do so, while an informal private trade is set up in selling water to low-income households. This ensures that international water companies will not bear losses from those who cannot afford to pay. It also has the propensity to make the poorest pay more than the well-to-do.

A small number of Western companies have taken over the supply of water to millions of people in the South, including the poorest city settlements. The World Bank and IMF have imposed the privatisation of water services on many countries, as a condition for granting loans.

> If governments try to terminate these contracts, they risk being sued. In the late 1990s, the World Bank and IMF demanded water privatisation in Cochamba, Bolivia, as a condition for debt relief and new loans. AdT, the consortium involved – partly owned by US-based Bechtel and Edison of Italy – was guaranteed profits in its 40-year contract with the government. Under AdT's management the price of water increased dramatically, to the point that it cost the average family living on the local minimum wage up to 25 per cent of its monthly income. Such unaffordable prices triggered huge public protests. The Bolivian government subsequently terminated the contract, and the companies involved attempted to sue the government for $25m. After huge public pressure and negative publicity, Bachtel dropped the case.[8]

World-wide, women and girls are responsible for domestic water provision. Men play little or no part in carrying water – water, as the supreme sustainer of life, is a substance associated with women. To render it inaccessible is an act of violence against them. More than 1.1 billion people in the world have no access to clean drinking water, an increasing proportion of them in the city slums. Water use by the urban poor is about 10 litres a day. In Britain, it is 135 litres a day. The people of Nairobi pay five times as much per litre as a citizen of North America.

Liberalisation, like all the other conventional wisdom of the Washington Consensus, marks a radical break with the theories of development which dominated from the 1950s to the 1970s. Governments are now expected to withdraw from the provision of public utilities. 'The right to water' is replaced by the management of water services. Water and sanitation are now supposed to be provided to 'consumers' for which they must pay at the local level. This cannot be reconciled with efforts to make drinking water universally available. *The Challenge of Slums* states that 'during the period of 1990 to 2000, the percentage of the world population with access to improved water services rose from 77 per cent to 82 per cent.'[9] The nature of this 'improvement' is not commented upon, and neither is the wave of privatisations and their impact upon such improvements.

Valuable observations on water and its availability are made by Gordon McGranahan and his colleagues in *The Citizens at Risk*.[10] The authors believe that, apart from access to clean drinking water (a basic necessity), quantity rather than quality of water also contributes to improvements in health. While piped water and articulated sewage remain largely unavailable, public investment declines and the private sector shows itself incapable of remedying these inadequacies, attention should turn to enhancing the supply, even of lower quality water.

Water contamination is only one aspect of the transmission of water-related disease. Apart from the ingestion of water-borne pathogens via contaminated drinking water, other water-related sicknesses do not require the same quality of water. People become infected because water has failed to carry pathogens away, and this can be helped by the volume of water. Other water-based transmission occurs through pathogens which spend part of their life-cycle in aquatic animals (schisto-somiasis and guinea-worm, for example), and through trans-mission by water-related insect vectors – malaria and dengue. Each requires different remedies: apart from clean drinking water, accessibility of domestic water, even of the non-potable kind; reduction of contact with infected water, and reduction of the contamination of surface waters – destroying the breeding-sites of insects and mosquitoes – are less costly and more prac-tical ways to improve health in poor urban areas.

Sylvy Jaglin, senior lecturer in Urban Geography at the Institut Francais d'Urbanisme at the University of Paris, describes three kinds of 'reform' in water provision, each depending upon the degree of integration of the target area into the market economy.[11] The water supply in capital cities is contracted out to international companies. Municipal water supplies are commercialised in other urban centres, with 'grassroots-level' contracting-out to user committees in poor and fringe-urban neighbourhoods. 'Participation' externalises some of the infrastructural and maintenance costs to user organisations. This form of involvement of poor people encourages them to organise, to give time and labour as well as monetary resources, in providing for their own communi-ties. Shared costs, local management systems and community action, seek to control the dynamics of participation and unite them with the dominant system, in order to assure universal access to water. This is a kind of apprenticeship of the poor to the ways of the market.

In Ouagadougou, the Burkina Faso government promised legalisation of tenure in slum areas if people shared the cost of installing and maintaining water provision. In Durban, private storage tanks were set up, so that individuals could control their own consumption and expenditure. Self-rationing and self-disconnecting are accomplished by poverty, and the issue of cut-offs becomes the responsibility of the penniless individual, not of the state or the company. The poor take responsibility for (or 'ownership' of, in the current jargon) their own poverty.

In Africa even by the early 1990s, water connections were below 50 per cent in most capital cities (except Dakar, with 60 per cent and Abidjan with 70 per cent).[12] Standpipes had been widely provided earlier, but these were closed down in the 1980s, in favour of private connections and small-scale selling-on of water. In urban areas, standpipes are increasingly used by companies, which license private operators to distribute water from them using a turncock employee. There has been an emergence of formal user associations, either as the main licensee of the facility, or as a local regulatory body representing the users, but the situation remains unsatisfactory, since neither system allows control over the decisions of public authorities or official suppliers. Complicity is not the same thing as participation. NGOs are sometimes used as mediators to make this system acceptable, but such 'partnerships' diffuse responsibility and legitimise new distribution of those responsibilities. While dominant companies concentrate on the affluent, the costs can be passed on through labyrinthine arrangements to the poorest and most vulnerable.

Fragmented and competitive forms of provision are now being recognised; alternative delivery systems can be set in place, rather than dismantling public provision and replacing it by private monopolies. But legalising local water markets and recognising private operators is not enough. Without regulation, this 'informal' economy has serious health risks. In

Ougadougou the poor pay five or six times more than those paying for the public service, and up to 20 times more in the event of seasonal shortages. In the early 1990s, 60 per cent of water from public standpipes was sold on.

Participation may assist wider access to water by enabling communal services to expand in areas that had no service previously, but it cannot make urban societies more equitable. The 'user pays' principle does not alter the capacity of richer communities to access more effective and safer supplies. Participation is not always a vector of institutional change.

Existing practice threatens to institutionalise standard services for the privileged, and palliative solutions for the poor. The urban poor are required, by 'participation' and charges, to pay for the installation and use of delivery systems which the well-to-do have always enjoyed at subsidised prices.

Box 9.2 An alternative to liberalisation: Porto Alegre

Most urban areas make extravagant claims for the desirability of their city. In the West, this is not difficult, since widespread prosperity has thrust many poor people to the periphery. This is why the success of the participatory budget programme of Porto Alegre, capital of Rio Grande do Sul in Brazil, has appealed so powerfully to those who wish to transform the sites of exploitation and misery which most cities of the South have become, despite their large tracts of affluence.

Porto Alegre was established in 1742 on the Guaibo River by migrants from the Azores. They were joined by further migrations from Germany, Italy and Poland. The city now has a population of about 1.3 million, with a further 3 million or so in adjacent areas. It is situated in rich agricultural land, and produces soya beans, leather, corned beef and rice. Although it is a prosperous city, in the late 1980s at least one-third of its people were still living in slums.

The 1988 Constitution of Brazil gave a percentage of national tax receipts to local authorities, and in 1989 the Workers' Party came to power in the city. Its greatest innovation was the idea of a participatory budget. Essentially, this meant that the people were able to determine the priorities in their area of local authority expenditure. By 2000, more than 40,000 people were taking part in the 16 popular assemblies held in local neighbourhoods, with professionals and people with particular expertise joining 'themed plenaries', in which particular issues were discussed – economic development, urban planning and transportation. Poor people turned out in significant numbers to take part. The system was intended primarily as an exercise of social inclusion, not as a way to maximising economic efficiency, although as it turned out, it proved to be both. The initiative has been copied by almost 200 municipalities in Brazil, and has inspired similar efforts all over the world. This has earned Porto Alegre an international reputation for innovative and transparent local government. One of the effects has been to divert resources towards the poorer sections of the urban population.

Budgets are weighted according to the demographic make-up of the urban areas, including density of population, the incidence of poverty, and lack of amenities. In 2000, 10 per cent of the poorest neighbourhoods were receiving 56 per cent of the budget allocated to housing, and as a result, there is virtually no squatting in the state of Rio Grande do Sul. The local authority turned down an offer by the Ford Company to locate a car plant in the area, since the inducements and infrastructural investments required could be deployed to better effect in city improvements. The construction of a five-star hotel was also rejected for similar reasons. In the ten years after 1989, sewerage and water was extended from 75 per cent of all dwellings in the city to 98 per cent, while the system of urban transport is one of the most effective in Brazil.

In 2004, the Workers' Party – which came to power at the centre in 2002 – lost control of the municipality of Porto Alegre, and power passed to the Social Democratic Party (PSDB), which promised to maintain the participatory budget and the transport system.

The greatest number of participants have come from the poorest neighbourhoods, and the result is seen in improvements in infrastructure in the places where this is most needed. In an article in the *New Internationalist*, Rebecca Abers stated, 'Contrary to the common assumption that civil society must strengthen before government will improve, in Porto Alegre a state-initiated policy that has encouraged civic organising has helped consolidate the new practices at all levels.'

Source: Rebecca Abers, *New Internationalist*, December 2002.

10
City borders

Of equal importance with migration in the growing population of cities is the enclosure of peripheral areas. The expansion of boundaries takes in former villages, transforms the use of agricultural land and alters the livelihood, not only of those already living there, but of the newcomers to suburban and near-urban areas.

How peripheral land is used varies. It may become a source of a different kind of farming, growing vegetables and livestock rather than wheat or rice, to feed the growing city. It may be a site for industrial estates, enclaves of high-tech specialised labour, or export-processing zones. It may be a location for luxury development for people escaping the social insecurity and breakdown of the inner city. It may be a dumping-ground for evictees from the slums. It may be the place chosen for infrastructural projects – an upgraded airport, a golf course, a park, a transport interchange.

Whatever happens, it means upheaval and change. Some gain while others lose. Urban development may follow the main transport routes out of town, along the main highways, but most cities simply redraw their boundaries in a wider circle around the urban hub.

The 'peri-urban interface' is the expression which indicates the merging of the city with the adjacent area, this explosive meeting ground of evictees of agricultural productivity and those ousted as a result of industrial efficiency.

The winners in the spreading city

While many small farmers lose out, urban interests with capital to invest can buy up land at low prices, often in collusive relationships with local governments and bureaucrats. Developers – 'colonisers', as they are sometimes, significantly, called – can erect speculative apartments for better-off citizens, or establish shopping malls or other private amenities in anticipation of future population growth.

There are also opportunities for great prosperity in areas adjacent to the city: farmers with access to credit in the peri-urban area, and who are capable of taking advantage of expanding city markets, may do very well indeed. They usually change from the production of staples – rice or wheat – to cereals, vegetables or livestock.

Rapid economic growth in the immediate hinterland of Hanoi has had a dramatic effect on farming communities.[1] Although the total acreage of land devoted to providing food has declined, more intensive land use has made it more productive. Pork, fish and vegetable production have increased, while rice has been reduced. At least one member of each family has usually gone into industry or service. Some have built houses for rent on their land, or have sold it to people from the city wanting to build their own houses.

Thanh Tri, adjacent to the built-up city area, has seen the fastest decline in land devoted to paddy (wet rice farming). Although housing, industry and infrastructure are eating into farmland, the land that remains is more intensively used for milk and vegetables. Farmers in the peri-urban area who can afford to do so, wait for land prices to rise or for compensation to be paid. As a result, 10 per cent of the land in the Thanh Tri is underused or left idle.

This district is downstream from the city's river. This brings pollutants from industry, and causes flooding, since new buildings and roads prevent rainwater from being absorbed by the earth. Low-lying ricefields are flooded, and the traditional two harvests have been reduced to one. Even the most negative consequences of development can be turned to good account, and some farmers turn the flooded fields into fishponds. In Thanh Tri, farming of fish and shrimps accounts for 20 per cent of the cultivated area. On one-third of this, the fish survive solely on nutrients from urban effluents and wastewater. The harmful components of urban waste are not removed to leave only those that can safely be used as fish nutrients. Some farmers combine fish farming with growing water-dependent vegetables such as spinach and morning glory. Water-hyacinths are grown for animal feed and composting.

In Thanh Tri, 80 per cent of households are agricultural, but many have at least one member in industry – electrical, fertilizer and battery factories – and this provides 30 per cent of the average household's income. Vegetable growing is lucrative, but requires extra labour, recruited from outlying rice-growing areas. Every change has repercussions elsewhere, sometimes nearby, sometimes at a medium distance, and occasionally in remote areas.

The change in land use over time is typically from two-harvest paddy to a single harvest, then to semi-permanent fishponds, and finally to landfill, which makes it ripe for urban construction.

In Thanh Tri, 13 per cent of land is taken up by housing, including existing villages and farmhouses. Although the villages are classified as 'conservation villages', they are rapidly being 'redeveloped' by owners, who replace single-storey buildings with apartment blocks, some for rent. They sometimes divide rural lots to sell to developers to generate funds for construction. Incomers to these villages are relatively well off, and the quality of building is superior. As Thanh Tri becomes more built up, the better-off will move on, and the villages be at risk of physical and social decay.

This characteristic development is dynamic and changing. Farmers around the city who provided vegetables may face stagnating prices for their produce, since growing city demand is answered by an increasing number of suppliers in ever-widening circles around the city. As infrastructure improves – precisely in order to convey goods to the urban market – more people enter the competitive race for providing these goods.

The villages of Lucknow

The village of Gangakhera is now within the city boundary of Lucknow.[2] The government negotiates with individual farmers to buy their land. It acquires land cheaply, since the farmers generally have no legal title to their land, although they have farmed it from time out of memory. The State Development Authority and the Lucknow Development Agency sell the land they acquire to developers, with whom they often have close commercial relationships.

A majority of residents of urban villages change, over time, from self-reliant farmers into unskilled labourers. Their loss of productive land effectively deprives them of their livelihood, and the compensation is derisory. The work opportunities for their children are limited. They become servants, drivers and security guards for newcomers who occupy land that was once theirs.

In a city like Lucknow, with its ancient courtly tradition, its extensive cantonment area (a legacy of the siege of 1857), its non-industrial culture, and focus on administration and small units devoted to *chikan* work (a form of traditional embroidery), there are few groups of organised poor. Land is a very sensitive issue in Lucknow, and a mere half-dozen NGOs (of more than 100) work in the urban sector.

Gangakhera is a tranquil collection of small houses and wheatfields, with winding roads following ancient patterns of land ownership. The old houses, of earth and wood, have largely been abandoned, and now provide shelter for animals. The people have moved into small concrete houses provided by the municipal authority. This has a profound impact on the way of living. Joint families have broken into smaller units, and each nuclear family has a separate kitchen. This is how people express the weakening of primary bonds that held families together – collective preparation of food represented symbolic commitment to the extended family group, and its dissolution is a significant step in the process of fragmentation.

Chota Lal, in his fifties, still works his land. He has not yet been approached by government authorities, so does not know his fate. He is aware that government is acquiring land, but is unaware of the rate of compensation. Chota Lal's family has no memory of ever having been anywhere else. He has five children, one boy and four girls. Two girls are married, and two remain at home. He would like them to study, but this is impossible. He defines his family as *khetibari* – agriculturists. They have always worked on their own land, although Chota Lal's son does so now reluctantly, knowing that time is running out. They produce *jowar* (or sorghum, a cereal), wheat and rice. Water has become a problem, for although handpumps have been installed in the fields, the water table has fallen as more and more water is extracted for other purposes, and water is out of reach of the pumps for much of the year. The unpredictable availability of water has subverted the family's livelihood.

Chota Lal will never sell his land voluntarily. 'When I am no more, it will be up to my children.' To him, land means freedom. He grows principally for family consumption, but when there is a surplus, he sells in the market. If the fields were linked to the canal and proper irrigation were possible, he could produce more. In recent years, the crop has been insufficient for the family's needs.

Chota Lal says people ask only that basic needs be fulfilled. He is unaware that this simple utterance is a form of blasphemy against the global market. He says:

> Just enough for survival. We don't want money. If you have money, you cannot sleep at night, you are wondering who is going to steal it. I have seen so many hardships. If I achieve a bare minimum that is more than enough. Even for my children, this minimum would be more than I have been able to do. I ask for nothing more, why should they?

The young men stand, arms around each other's shoulder, smiling the superior smile of youth. Of course they want to leave the village. They have been to school, up to tenth or twelfth standard. They will find work, in government service, or some private company, shop, something clean that befits their new status, their non-agricultural urban sensibility. This altered state of mind shows in the clothes they wear, the way their hair is styled. The future is before them. Their hope – and indeed, expectation – is palpable. Their lives are moving away from agriculture towards the lights of the city.

In such places, an ancient peasant obstinacy confronts the dynamism of urban life, economic growth and social upheaval. The only constant in this turbulent process is that the poor continue to be cheated. The old men believe their honesty, their labour and their age will preserve them from developments that are about to dispossess them of everything they have known. This may also be the fate of most of their children, the laughing young men who think they can conquer the city, when they and their energies will be used up by forces of which they have little more understanding than their parents.

Gangakhera is characteristic of many ancient settlements which have been absorbed by the spreading city. Such villages, which have grown to serve agriculture, are not reorganised according to the needs of the city. Basic services become more scarce and inadequate over time, and the villages, overgrown and crowded, turn into slums. The people of the villages, deprived of their traditional livelihood, are forced into unskilled work, and their opportunities for self-improvement are worsened, not enhanced, by the city environment. Former agricultural workers and their children are made more vulnerable by the city which has caught them up in its unmerciful embrace.

Pressure on the peri-urban area: relocation of the poor

Pressure on the rural hinterland of the city also comes from the relocation of people from the crowded central city districts. *The Challenge of the Slums* states that wholesale evictions of slum dwellers have now been 'discredited', and largely discontinued.[3] In spite of this, the practice of removing them from the site of their livelihood is still widely practised. In large cities, communities of poor people have long departed the core area, apart from pockets under bridges, flyovers and on parcels of hazardous or polluted land. Many evictions now take place from areas that might have been perceived as peripheral 20 years ago, but which are now well within city borders.

Raghubir Nagar was a slum in West Delhi, close to a large private hospital. This community had evolved a form of barter, which served the people of the area well, and was itself a survival of older rural practices. People bought household vessels of tin and plastic, and offered them to middle-class householders in the neighbourhood in return for second-hand clothing. The slum dwellers washed, repaired and pressed the garments and sold them. With the profit from this, they were able to make a tolerable living, and to invest in new vessels to exchange for further clothing in the vicinity. This represented a spontaneous form of conservation and recycling. The people asked for nothing but to be left to pursue this useful activity in peace.

As employment in the formal sector (government services, administration, state-owned industry) has contracted, through privatisation, mechanisation and cuts in public spending, the percentage of people working in this area has declined, so that in India it is now well below 10 per cent. The urban poor must create their own work, in an ever-expanding and increasingly ingenious informal sector. But as the fate of the people of Raghubir Nagar shows, these activities are also under constant pressure, and the source of their hard-won livelihood is liable to be wiped out at any time.

The Delhi authorities think of themselves as progressive, as is doubtless proper for a capital city which is also one of the ten largest in the world. They have provided flyovers for motorists, and vast excavations of the city for the Metro system. They have encouraged five-star hotels, and developers who have built extensively housing, entertainment and shopping facilities for the city's middle class.

This generosity does not extend to the poor. The people of Raghubir Nagar were evicted with little warning and less cere-mony in 2001. Their huts were broken and they were lucky to escape with a few belongings. They were dumped 15 kilometres away, on a desolate, treeless wasteland on the far periphery of Delhi, a place called Bakerwala, without amenities and without shelter. They were offered allotment slips, for plots of 12 or 18 square yards, for which they had to pay Rs7000 (US $160). Many borrowed money to pay for this; some, appalled by the demand for an impossible sum, moved to another informal settlement. Those who went to Bakerwala had to mortgage the slips to private moneylenders, at an interest rate of 5 per cent per month, so they could build houses. They are doubly – and for most, irretrievably – in debt.

Since removal disrupted their livelihood, their chances of repaying their debts are slim. The best most people can hope for is intermittent employment, mainly on construction, at Rs70 or 80 daily (about US$1.70).

Since the relocation, the site has been improved. There is still no access road, and vehicles slide and skid through the muddy potholes. Once arrived at the settlement, people are astonished to see paved streets on a grid pattern, drains running with grey wastewater, and lines of drooping concrete lamp-posts. This infrastructure is a result of work by Jagriti Mahila Samiti, Women's Awakening, which has fought on behalf of the urban poor, especially widows and abandoned wives in the community. The Samiti took the Delhi Municipal Corporation to court for failing to spend the money allocated for infrastructure according to the law. At the time of the eviction, Nirmala Sharma, of the Samiti, was beaten up by the police and locked in a temple. Her assistant, Durdana, was also detained and mistreated.

The result is an incongruous township, with a wide range of structures. There are some single-storey one-room brick buildings, while others have a second storey. There are bare plots, with shelters of polythene and wood, where the poorest remain.

In the crowd that gathers, no one will say conditions here are an improvement on the slum they left. 'How can it be better with no means of livelihood?' asks Dharan Singh. Some say they will be forced to sell the houses they have constructed and move back into the city. 'There, we used to eat three times a day. Here, we have learned the meaning of hunger once more.' In Raghubir Nagar women found work as domestics. Half a kilometre away, a new speculative development of eight-storey apartment blocks is visible, but these remain largely unoccupied because the area is remote.

The village of Bakerwala is a long-settled community – a street of ancient houses, ragged wasting fields of wheat, and the vestiges of rural life. Plots of land will rise in value and make sale almost irresistible. Where city meets village, neither is advantaged: slum dwellers are evictees, while villagers feel invaded. The resentment is reflected in the reluctance of teachers to enrol the children of the new-comers in the schools. 'They call us dirty and idle.' Lalitha, a serious girl who does not know her age, tells how difficult it has been to gain admission into the government school. The teachers extort fees, claiming the school is meant only for the original village inhabitants. The school is in any case under-resourced, with only two or three teachers, when at least twice as many are required.

Lack of amenities cuts into social customs and expecta-tions. There is no temple, no mosque, no cremation or burial ground for the dead. There is no hospital, and the dispensary scarcely functions. When doctors do show up, they treat the residents with contempt, and the necessary medicines are rarely available. If someone falls ill at night, there is nowhere to go. Of course, private doctors are present: but their qualifi-cations are sometimes suspect, and they require a fee of Rs50 for a consultation.

Some have abandoned the site and gone back to their former workplace. There are two particularly poignant features of this forsaken spot. One is the heroism of women's efforts to survive. Jithu tells how she returns daily to Raghubir Nagar to continue the barter trade in vessels and clothing. She gets up at 2.00 a.m. and prepares food for her five daughters and two sons, leaving in a private van at 3.30 a.m. for her place of labour. She pays Rs10 for the fare, and Rs5 for her *tokri*, or basket of freshly cleaned clothes. Sometimes she takes her son, which costs her a further Rs10, so the daily fare reaches almost half her Rs100 earnings.

They reach the market at 4.00 a.m., and wait for the traders who buy the clothes. By 8.00 a.m. they are free to eat breakfast. Then the rounds to the houses begin, carrying the vessels and exchanging them for old clothing. This continues all day. Jithu arrives home at 8.30 or 9.00 p.m. The children help prepare supper, but by the time household chores are finished it is 10.30 p.m., and she sleeps for a few hours before rising again at 2.00 a.m. On bad days, she may not have the fare to come home at all, so sleeps in the open air market. Outside her house, the trousers, shirts, blouses and sarees she has pressed and cleaned are drying in the sun. Like many people here, she is from Gujarat, where small-scale farmers were displaced by persistent drought.

A second touching feature is that among the majority of competent, hard-working people, some are very talented. Indraj, a middle-aged man, is an artist, a mask-maker, but there is no call for his skills. There are many musicians, singers and artists among the people; none of them are employed.

People are isolated even from the symbols of authority. They make shift as best they can, using their considerable powers of invention to survive. They came to the city in search of a livelihood they could no longer procure at home, only to find themselves evicted once more from their fragile community, and made poor again – this time, by the very place in which they had sought relief from their poverty.

There are thousands of places like this on the edge of cities. These relocations are not merely evictions, but are also coercive efforts to compel people into a market economy, without the resources to operate in it successfully. The result is indebtedness, to extortionate private moneylenders, NGO microcredit (small loan) schemes or banks. Although bondage still persists in rural areas, and is sometimes paid for in lifelong labour, the city is by no means always a place of liberation, since it too produces forms of debt-dependency.

11
The country and the city

The relationship between city and country is complex. The hinterland of cities can be very wide indeed, as any extensive slum reveals. In Mumbai's Dharavi, there are communities from as far away as Kerala, Bengal, Gujarat and Orissa, while migrants from Karnataka or Maharashtra have reconstituted whole settlements, mock 'villages' in the city. The world's richest cities can, of course, command resources from a hinterland that is truly global. Out-of-season fruits and vegetables are available at any time in New York or Tokyo; oil can be drawn from where time and nature have created it and transferred to the thirst engines of global mobility; while the best brains of the world can be bought to service the economies of the USA or Western Europe.

The attitudes of urban dwellers to the countryside are determined by the relationships they maintain with their place of origin. Many who have acquired land, either in a village or on a periphery that has been enclosed by the city, started city life as hawkers or vendors. These occupations cover a wide range of activities, as may be seen from an even cursory view of central city markets. These local markets are under growing threat from global markets, which little by little displace them, although local produce consumed close to where it is grown or made remains the principal source of gain. Of course, even the local market of a city like Bangalore calls upon produce from a considerable distance. To the surrounding countryside, even the city is a kind of *imperium*, a global market in embryo, setting producers against each other and influencing what is grown hundreds of kilometres away.

Many young people see the city as an escape from the conformism of rural life. As people grow older, they may develop a kind of double life, with one foot in the village and another in the city. Those who become very successful and make a lot of money, invest in land. This may be a prudent way of increasing their wealth, or for the middle class, of buying into the countryside as a place of relaxation and recreation. They buy a farm, for holidays and weekends, so that children can play freely, and they too lead a life that straddles both rural and urban, although for them it is not a question of material survival. Long-distance commuters, as in the West, try to get the best of both worlds.

Small urban contrasts

Between 50 per cent and 75 per cent of urban populations live in small or intermediate centres, many of which are also growing very rapidly, although their problems are overshadowed by the more dramatic spread of the great cities. This is particularly true of India and China. A population of more than a quarter of a million constitutes a large town; between 20,000 and 250,000 is intermediate, whereas towns of less than 20,000 are small. These rough-and-ready demarcations give little idea of the diverse nature of those cities: Hardoy and Satterthwaite point out that some are regional market centres, while others are intensively developed industrial villages.[1] These have a closer relationship with the countryside than that of big cities.

Research into mobility patterns and rural–urban relationships was undertaken in a low-income neighbourhood on the edge of Mombasa in Kenya and a rural settlement, Kilifi, 60 kilometres away.[2] The researchers focused particularly on the mobility of mothers moving between the village and a poor district of the city.

In the city some kind of self-employment is possible, and earnings help the rural household. Services like health care and education are within reach. If you own a house, renting a room is lucrative. But everything costs money – food, water, firewood, housing. Saving is difficult. There is no security if you live on government land. The environment is poor and overcrowded. There is more illness, and competition is fierce when everyone is trying to make a living in the same way. Finding work is hard for women with young children. Married women depend on their husbands, and unmarried women may have to sleep with a man to get a place to stay.

The high male/female ratio in the urban population is because men tend to move to the city once their schooling is finished. Women go to the city to stay with their husbands and earn, but return home to give birth and care for children, and to maintain the family farm. Many boys remain in the rural areas when mothers move to town: 50 per cent of girls and 65 per cent of boys go to primary school in the rural area, but in the secondary school this falls to 10 per cent of girls and 45 per cent of boys.

Variations of this survival pattern occur all over Africa. The stereotyping of rural migrants to the city as disoriented or isolated is misleading. Many know well the environment into which they are moving. The breakdown of the extended family is overestimated: it has more resilience through time and space than has been understood. There is continuous exchange between the two areas – rural and urban information, customs, practices and ideas, as well as goods. Survival is not a matter of individual salvation: the maintenance of the integrity of the family is the overriding purpose. This also eases the harshness of urban living conditions, which shock many outsiders.

Urban farmers

From studies by the International Development Research Centre (IDRC) between 1983 and 1993, it emerged that some 67 per cent of Nairobi's urban families are farmers, but only 29 per cent of them produce food within the city boundaries.[3] In some cities, one-quarter of families claim that self-produced food is indispensable to their survival. Many urban families survive by splitting their time between the city and a homestead. In Nairobi only 7 per cent of people keep livestock in the city – mainly chickens – but far more do so in their village *shamba* (field or allotment).

It is estimated that 70 per cent of the poultry and eggs eaten in Kampala, Uganda, are produced within the city. The nutritional status of children in Kampala in families which produce some of their own food is significantly higher than in those who buy everything in the market. Few recent migrants to the city grow their own food, since they do not have access to land.

The majority of urban farmers are women – in Kenya 62 per cent are. Of these, 64 per cent are heads of household. The IDRC found that only 41 per cent of the urban families in Kenya owned the land they farmed, whereas 42 per cent were using government land. Where urban land that has been controlled by government is privatised, this may reduce the opportunities for food production.

In Lagos, commercial vegetable enterprises are carried on within the city limits. The majority of these entrepreneurs are male, and the primary occupation of almost half is farming. Most are in-migrants from other states. It is a dry-season activity, from October to March, when demand in Lagos is high. Among the crops are green amaranths, cabbage, spinach, roselle and water leaf. Non-leafy vegetables include aubergines, cucumbers, spring onions and radishes. The average size of a plot is 1400 square metres. Two or three crops of leafy vegetables can be harvested in a single season. The sites are rented from the local authority for six months, after which people go back to their home areas for arable farming. Most farmers employ share-croppers to help with the work, and these receive 10 per cent of the harvest. Inputs come from local markets, and organic manure from poultry farms – also a city-based activity.

The chief immediate obstacles to urban vegetable production are lack of access to land, to credit and appropriate technologies. Because farmers do not have the right to use the land and may be summarily evicted, they are discouraged from investing in permanent structures. Without concrete-walled wells, they have to work to re-excavate the existing hand-dug wells several times a season. Produce is also liable to be stolen, and rubbish dumped on the site. It remains a provisional, temporary occupation.

Urban farmers play an increasing part in the provision of nutritious food to urban people who are vulnerable to malnourishment and ill-health in an oppressive city environment. If land were secure, vegetable producers could form cooperative groups, and could get loans from agricultural credit institutions.[4]

Neglect of small centres

Paul Jenkins defined the 'rural–urban interface' in Mozambique and Angola by looking at three urban centres, Mocuba and Montepuez in Mozambique and Huambo in Angola.[5] Angola is about 40 per cent urban, Mozambique 34 per cent. He showed that global forces are major determinants of the fate of small towns, even though such communities appear marginal in the great drama of globalisation. Supra-national action is required to counteract stagnation in peripheral areas, since the global context limits the possibilities for local action.

Urbanisation means different things to various disciplines – the planner, environmentalist, economist, sociologist and anthropologist. It is essentially a process. The researchers use five criteria to judge the position of the household on the rural–urban continuum: monetary penetration, labour activity, access to sociocultural resources, access to physical resources and legal-political involvement. They speak of the urban–rural 'frontline', a term taken from warfare.

The colonial period demanded unskilled labour in urban areas, which has been bypassed in the era of globalism. State agriculture and the demand for private farm labour have also decayed. Export-led agriculture has been undermined by lack of investment, falling commodity prices, and continuing subsidies in the rich world. The dominance of South Africa in the region is a further constraint on development. One result is urbanisation by default, the growth of towns without employment – a phenomenon which also affects major cities. Wars have destroyed much rural infrastructure and driven people into urban centres. The urban township of the colonial period, and the peri-urban squatter settlements of post-independence, have been augmented by linear village development along main roads. Within the township and peri-urban areas, livelihoods have also changed, and there is a mixture of urban and rural economic activities.

Small urban areas like these are seeing substantial population growth with a limited economic basis. This frontline of urbanisation responds to changing macroeconomic influences. The economy was previously defined by colonial export-oriented production, but post-independence policy focused on internal production. Economic development is now largely determined by globalism, which has a specific demand for low-cost, relatively high-skilled labour. Mining and manufacturing have shifted to where natural resources are easier to extract and skilled labour is more easily available. The commercial basis for agriculture has been affected, hitting small and medium urban centres hard. Rural development options are reduced, especially while Western countries continue to subsidise their own agriculture.

Even subsistence-level activities have been destroyed by civil war; and export opportunities for both agricultural products and manufactures have been wiped out by cheap goods and food from abroad. Urban centres now service elites, with wealth filtering down minimally to the poor through informal markets. Displaced people who want to return to their rural roots find themselves hampered by mines, lack of infrastructure (roads, bridges, wells) and limited markets. Part of their livelihood strategy must now be located in urban areas.

Previously, peri-urban populations were the product of labour markets with some opportunity for upward mobility. Now peri-urban areas in sub-Saharan African cities are dumping grounds, where households depend upon both urban and rural sources of income to eke out a bare survival. This also leads to the development of peri-rural areas – large villages which grow up around markets and transport junctions.

This is not urbanisation based on a strong demand for labour, but urbanisation based on a strong rejection of labour. In this context, urban land management will have to accept intermediary forms of land access based on 'informal' but widely legitimate practices, neither fully 'modern' or 'urban', nor 'traditional or 'rural'. Hybrid cultures arise: livelihood strategies are the basis for poverty reduction, and these must bestride both rural and urban areas. Here we see the impact on the rural areas of the dual global culture, which seeks higher productivity, dispensing with labour both in agriculture and industry.

Mozambique and Angola provide dramatic examples of problems which are common, though they vary in severity, throughout the developing world. Macroeconomic forces concentrate wealth relatively unchecked, while the traditional defenders of the poor – governments – are undermined. The result is expanding peri-urban (and peri-rural areas), especially at the global economic periphery. Local solutions are all very well, but cannot be provided in isolation from global realities, and policies which are internationally coordinated.

The tedium of the provincial town

Even with populations swollen by rural migrants, many provincial centres in the South – some of them quite substantial – are places of languor and boredom, especially for young people educated out of agriculture, but with no immediate prospect of urban employment. I recall the youth of Korat in Thailand, Cebu in the Philippines, Barisal in Bangladesh, waiting, always waiting to depart, to leave for the capital, to get a job abroad, for something to happen.

The landscapes of provincial towns in the developing world are often grim. Barisal has pocked ramshackle buildings, unfinished brickwork bleeding onto the street, monsoon-stains and holes in the road, and a greenish pond in the centre of town with rusty railings. At the bus terminal ancient battered vehicles throw out their mushroom of pollution, waiting for the roofs to be loaded with local produce destined for the regional capital. Weatherbeaten market women sit with bundles of tomatoes, live chickens in wicker cages or evil-smelling *dourian* fruit. In the town centre, there are a statue of a writer who was born there and went on to become a national poet, another of a liberation hero, memorials to independence and to those fallen in wars that are almost forgotten.

Above the streets, there are the sagging tangled lines of telephone wires, wound around ceramic spools on concrete poles, and wilting street lamps that throw a pale orange lustre onto the evening crowds. The market tends to be animated in the evening, as the daily wage-earners go with their money to buy vegetables for supper. There is a crude barber's saloon, with a high wooden chair. The men talk about crop prices, rainfall, or the chances of work on the new bridge that is going to cut the travel time to the regional capital. The women traders on the sidewalk wait hours for customers, talking of the rising price of necessities or the shocking suicide of a farmer who couldn't repay his loan, and who killed his wife and children before taking his own life.

The town, although not old, looks worn and tired. There is a half-finished civic building begun by a political party which lost power, so it was never completed and rusty reinforcing rods protrude from the concrete. An occasional villa is occupied by returnees from abroad, with lights winking around a doorway carved from ancient rosewood. The neglected fruit trees on the hillside no longer inspire a tremor of anticipation in the young as the mango season approaches. The shops with videos and music-cassettes bring other excitements – not only devotional songs and ancient US Westerns, and the latest Bollywood film-music, but also pornography for the unofficial video-parlour behind the shop in the small central market.

The shops offer limited goods: wedding jewellery, clocks, plastic bowls and aluminium vessels, bolts of coloured cloth. There are repair shops with dismembered car chassis, battered television sets, buckled bicycles; a dry-goods store with jute sacks full of beans, pulses and rice of variable quality; and shops selling Western goods – Maggi soups, Nestlé chocolate, Lipton's tea, Lever Brothers soaps and shampoos, children's toys, hairslides, ribbons and skipping ropes. Everything is makeshift and second-rate. These are goods to console failure, immobilism and lack of ambition.

The provincial town is marked by absences: the departures of those who have gone in search of a better life. Daughters go to the garment factories of the capital city, sons to college, fathers to the Gulf to become drivers, gardeners or shop assistants in the emporia of Jeddah or Dubai. Mothers are called away from their families to domestic service, or possibly the sex industry. These are places depleted of energy, waiting for remittances, gifts, a return.

Perhaps this is why the river launch terminal, the bus stand and the railway station are the sites of greatest energy. These are also the places from which the produce of the area departs, and through which the wealth is filtered. Rice, jute, fruit, vegetables, cotton, cacao, coffee, flowers and manufactured goods sit in big metal containers, bound for harbours and railway junctions that link up with a remote elsewhere.

The provincial towns speaks of a spare sufficiency, of people working increasingly for an unfair exchange for the goods or materials they produce. It is a provisional place, a transit for refugees and evictees of agriculture. It is a jumble of unplanned iron, cement, stone, rust and mildew, worn threadbare by the feet of too many departures, a place visited only by transients and those who have come to take something more from the injured people, to rob them of more land, more energy, more produce at unfair prices.

The provincial town is also for some a place of longing. Once separated from the necessities of land, its ceremonies and rituals, its inevitable patterns of sowing, growing, ripeness and harvest, the people themselves become a kind of cash crop, in whose hearts new needs and desires take root. They are touched by a desire for small luxuries, relief from the remorselessness of a labour no longer attended by a collective dance and joyful feast at the successful completion of the winnowing of the rice and cutting of the corn. Instead they are consoled by small comforts on sale from the shops and stores – the sweetness of chocolate, the colour of lipstick, the scent of soap, sandalwood or lavender. These small wants are nourished by the money in hand, and come to express themselves in a need for new stimulants, new forms of escape – the drink fermented from rice or banana leaves, the cough-mixture which raises the spirits, or the flesh which is forbidden, the painted eyes and seductive smile in the tin-built brothel.

But above all, there is the desire to escape, just as people have escaped the fields, where they stood with their ankles in water. They resent the relentless labour of collecting fuel, eyes watering with smoke from cooking fires, lungs filled with the acrid smoke from the only wood that remains in the depleted woods. The town echoes with the rhythmic tread of boots in the early morning on the rough road to the cigarette factory, the sawmill, the canning plant, the scrapyards where the metal from ancient tankers is dismantled, the factories where the Juki machines hum their music of drudgery. The clothes accumulate in the dispatch area: parka jackets with imitation fur for the winters of Canada, sequin-sewn spangles for jeans that will dance the night through in the discos of San Francisco, the shoes with impossible heels that will walk through the glass and marble palaces of Manhattan, floral dresses that will float on the summer breezes of Copenhagen or Turin.

The faltering economic role of these bloated market centres – whose purpose was to serve as an exchange for goods produced and consumed locally – has transformed them into repositories of exotic objects which come from afar, which stir the imagination and sow dissatisfaction in the heart of those who are just beginning the journey from a ruined subsistence existence into the mysterious glittering caverns of a global market. The subjective experience of the people of the towns and cities does not exist independently of its location in the economic charts and mappings of a global economy. If we do not include this in any discussion of the formation of towns and cities, we miss a vital element in the great movements of people, summoned to the long march of globalisation.

12
The triumph of the middle class

The city belongs, overwhelmingly, to an increasingly conspicuous middle class. Transformed cities in South Korea, Malaysia, China and India, and in Central and South America, bear the imprint of an expansive urban middle class and its demand for more living space. Apartment blocks and fortified communities of privilege have demolished much slum housing, and overshadowed that which remains. In cities with a significant – say 20 per cent – proportion of the middle class and rich, it is they who dominate the cityscape. Where poor people remain in central areas, these are usually hazardous sites – areas prone to flooding, close to fetid canals and polluted ponds, on steep slopes, at risk from both natural and industrial hazards They are often bypassed by the new expressways, flyovers, offices and shopping malls which form the central nucleus of the modern city – the citadel as it once might have been, defended in this enlightened age, not from outside marauders, not from barbarians and aliens, but from its own poor.

The 'disappearance' of the poor

The makeover of the city environment, with its symbols of modernity – high-rises and golf courses, enclosures of hotels and clubs – has led to a curious paradox: the 'disappearing' of the urban poor at a time when they have never been more numerous. The imagery of the city, the postcards framing its most celebrated views, embodies images of the presidential palace, the towering mountain, the clustered skyscrapers at the commercial 'heart' (that symbol of the heartless city), the flood-lit historical monuments, parliament buildings, temples, churches or mosques, and even, in less sophisticated centres, pictures of national dignitaries opening the first flyover or ring road.

As the numbers of the urban poor grow, governments spend less on services, privatisations demand cost recovery for the amenities provided, the danger to health increases and livelihoods become more perilous, the ousting of the poor by market forces (as opposed to the military forces who performed the same function 20 years ago) gives them dwindling visibility. Though true of most of the developing world, it is less true of much of Africa, where more than 90 per cent of city populations live in slums, from the bleak stony *kebeles* of Addis Ababa and the shanties of N'Djamena, to 60 per cent or more in Dar es Salaam and Lagos. In Africa, despite enclaves of luxury, the omipresence of the white vehicles of aid agencies and international institutions, five-star hotels in which businessmen and women conspire to take control of whatever resources remain, the poor still dominate the city.

The modern landscape

The cities of the middle class have been systematically landscaped. The last thing governments want to display is ancient twisted thoroughfares with tin shacks and rocky roads. The chaotic vendors and hucksters in the old market quarter, the countrywomen with their headloads of bananas, papaya, cucumbers or oranges, block the traffic on dusty paths, and get in the way of those trying to reach the more urgent locations of labour that belong to the aerial connections of globalism – air conditioned offices, cool retail malls, young women in department stores who are flawlessly groomed and worthy of the articles they sell. Sometimes 'traditional' market areas and old quarters have been sanitised and turned into a tourist attraction for exotic guests, and eyesores are changed into amenities.

Tourism and business travel have left their conspicuous mark on cities. Hotels create private enclosures of luxury. They are used not only by gilded transients, but also by local elites, for weddings, parties, business conferences and receptions for advisers and experts from international financial institutions and donor agencies. Tourists, a major source of foreign exchange, move between hotels and the city 'sights' in observation coaches. Even those en route for coastal resorts spend at least a couple of days in the capital or main regional centre. The road from the airport becomes a primary object of 'beautification' (the official policy of the ugliest cities in the world), with the result that it is lined with rows of oleanders and embellished with advertisements for skin-bleach or Mazda cars. They conceal the leprous concrete and dusty polythene roofs of huts in the marshy area beneath the causeway.

Just as garment factories have changed all the cities where they have nested in the same way, so a global middle class has altered the cities of the South after an identical pattern. This is not only because the middle class occupy a disproportionate share of the land, but because their workplaces, their leisure and shopping habits have generated a vast volume of vehicular traffic, to get them from the downtown area to their residential complexes.

This has led to the building – often financed by scarce public money, sometimes through private development of tollways – of expressways and elevated motorways that cut through residential and agricultural land, rising triumphantly on stilts over ancient public spaces and living areas, dipping into grassy cuttings and tunnelling under landmarks that it is impossible to demolish. Inscribed on the face of the city is the elsewhere that is the destination of the rich. They escape into new compounds, ziggurats of luxury dwellings, secluded compounds of villas and private super-markets, parkland and swimming pools. The city is demar-cated, partitioned, divided into that most persistent of apartheids – between rich and poor.

The construction industry draws workers from rural areas, sometimes from neighbouring, even poorer countries, to sites where huge metal cranes, clumsy prehistoric birds, prey on the earth-bound people below. Most new construction is commer-cial and residential. The workers' quarters are temporary structures of corrugated tin, wood or bamboo, dormitories of infernal heat and discomfort. Whole families live for years in these places, women washing clothes in a bowl of discoloured water, children playing in the dust and bricks broken by their older brothers and sisters for foundations and road-building. Workers' hutments pose a strong contrast to the idealised panels of artists' impressions of the new condominium – soar-ing structures called Seagull Towers or Mountjoy Apartments, bathed in perpetual sunlight and surrounded by a greenery rarely seen outside botanical gardens.

Roads and distances

Road networks convey people to where they work or shop, or are entertained in cafes, restaurants, night-clubs and boutiques. Roads are the most effective agents of perpetual clearances of the poor – the long historical continuity of evictions of those who occupy land wanted for more urgent purposes. Many of an earlier middle class, whose bunga-lows, often inherited or copied from colonial occupiers, sprawled on languid seafronts and spacious avenues of rain-trees, have sold them to developers. In their place condos rise, whose occupants can sip Singapore slings and gaze dreamily at dhows and fishing-boats on the horizon.

In the suburb of south Delhi where I stay, there are at least half a dozen jewellery stores: magnificent palaces of glass and marble, where families sit beneath chandeliers examining chunky and unattractive gold ornaments, decorations, anklets, bangles and jewellery spread out on red velvet cushions, attended by funereal and subdued sales personnel. Expensive shops offer fabrics and clothing and shoes bearing the logos of transnational companies, some of it made in smoky tenements in the same city, places more remote to their buyers than the travel-poster advertisements for Dubai and Paris. Chinese restaurants serve culinary delicacies confected of monosodium glutamate and chilli.

Expansive billboards advertise lotteries and get-rich schemes, cigarettes associated, not with death, but with glamour and freedom. In the cafes, while one-day cricket internationals play on giant screens, rap music at high volume accompanies the conversations of sleek young people, which rarely stray from the cost of their latest purchases, and are permanently interrupted by the birdsong of mobile phones. The middle class are a visibly lucrative cash-crop: intensively cultivated by the market, they produce simultaneous multiple harvests of profit, eating and listening to music, shopping and talking to absent friends.

The relation of the middle class to the poor of the city is similar to that of the West to the global middle class; that is to say, the middle class are objects of envy and emulation. Their lifestyles embody the aspirations of those who have little or nothing; and in their present, the city narrative embodies the future of all. Poor people have only to accept the model proposed by privilege, and to acquiesce in the silent authority of the universal market.

The affluent image

The affluence and influence of the middle class dominate, not only the city, but equally the image of the country in the world. India, formerly represented by the begging bowl, is now perceived as a pioneer of high-tech and a reservoir for outsourcing by Western-based transnationals. Most cities contain shining enclaves of 'the modern sector' – dedicated IT parks, business districts, ring roads and of course, protected communities.

This changes the image of the country from victim to threat: its people are going to filch the jobs of US and UK workers, the competitors and rivals of globalism. The affluent, not the poor, now speak for India. This creates the impression that poverty is a residual problem. Similarly in China, the cities eclipse inequality, the wretchedness and despair of the rural areas, the poisonings of the elements of existence in the damaged hinterlands. The majestic towers of Shanghai, the instant growth of Pudong with its biggest shopping mall in Asia, and the Jin Mao Tower, third tallest building in the world, dazzle the eye, and distract from the conditions in which goods from China are actually manufactured.

Imports to the West of toys, apparel and basic household items are seen as usurping the capacity of the West to produce even the most basic necessities. The industriousness and entrepreneurial capacity of the Chinese middle class have taken over symbolic representation of the country, displacing the ancient hapless victims of flood and famine. The dynamic cities are emblems of global transformation, and serve both to illuminate and to obscure the complexity of the real relationships contained within them, and the relationships between themselves, the countryside and the rest of the world. They demonstrate what Saskia Sassen describes as 'the insertion of the global in the national', which constitutes a 'partial and incipient denationalisation'.[1] The conspicuous skylines of the cities are emblems of those functions of national economies which belong elsewhere and everywhere. This does not take Pudong out of China, but its economic function is part of a re-territorialising of the world.

The spaces of the middle class city speak of prosperity and progress. These too are diverse and tiered. There remains a strict hierarchy of privilege, and they do not tell of the ways in which the psychic landscapes of the people have been restructured. For these, too, have been thoroughly reconstructed.

The sensibility of the middle classes

It is an old story that in the early industrial era, the sensibility of the peasantry was broken and re-made in the image of mass manufacture. Arguments about whether the standard of living rose between the 1790s and the 1840s remain unresolved. E. P. Thompson stated that even if most people's income rose during the period, the sense of subjective loss made them feel impoverished.[2] The violent compulsions of industrialism were coercive and destructive of a familiar world, so that the experience was of disruption and falling standards, even though objectively it may be true that far more wealth than ever before had been created in Britain.

Similar mechanisms are at work in the South today; and they affect people in the vanguard of transformation, the middle classes who are the undisputed beneficiaries of globalisation, its most shining examples and advocates. This they certainly are, but as they are drawn into new relationships with the outside world, the psychological, emotional and spiritual costs do not figure in the deductions on the printout of their salary chits.

In other words, those advantaged by urbanisation, modernisation and development pay a price beyond that of their new apartments, their sleek cars, their fashionable clothes, their mobility and participation in the global economy. If there are problems, these are a matter of 'transitional frictions', trivial compared with the material improvements they enjoy. And the theory persists that these will, in time, be transmitted to the rest of the population.

Even the assault on the traditional culture and identity of the people of China, Brazil or India does not immediately register on monitors that record only indices of rising living standards. Yet changes in relationships, in family structure, in how people interpret purpose and meaning, alter and corrode the daily lives of people. They must adapt themselves to epic shifts in the way their lives mesh with others, including those attached to them by blood, kinship and physical location. And they are expected to make their own private accommodation with the consequences of globalisation.

Growing inequalities between rich and poor lead to closed communities, new spatial segregations, new sites of 'self-reliance', in which everything is provided. The well-to-do emerge only in private transport on their way to equally protected environments, where they work, shop, relax and socialise.

Box 12.1 The mistress as maid

Luisa lives in a villa in Sao Paulo, fortified by fancy wrought-iron grilles and a high wall. It has security guards in two military-looking towers. Her home has the aspect of an ornamental prison. Her husband is a banker, and her two children are weekly boarders at a private school. She herself goes out in a chauffeur-driven car to lunch meetings with friends, charity committee meetings, concerts, and social events with her husband. She yearns to go out alone and mingle with the crowds she normally sees only from behind the tinted glass of the car.

Occasionally she will take the bus into the city; and on such occasions, she says that she *dresses like her maid*. She removes all jewellery, and puts on a plain dress she has acquired specifically for the purpose of disguise as a poor woman. She worries that the white spaces on her arms where her watch and bracelets have been might alert potential criminals to her identity as a rich woman. Her excursions into the city are both exciting and disturbing. The frustration at being cut off from people – her mother worked as saleswoman in a department store – together with her fear of violent crime, create a tension she finds impossible to resolve.

Source: personal communication.

Luisa's story (see Box 12.1) reflects a fairly minor conflict in the game of survival as a rich person in a city where a majority are poor and believed to be predatory. But it is not the physical arena at all where the real adjustments are made.

The ideology of individualism reaches more deeply into the psyche of privilege. The need to pursue a demanding professional and personal life sets up new struggles between duty and inclination, and strains to the limit ancient bonds of kinship, family and connectedness to others. This struggle draws both women and men of the middle class into choices which (perhaps because they are not really choices at all) leave a residue of guilt and shame, since they often infringe customary duties towards loved ones.

Career against care

Many relatively privileged people in the South believe that their social values can resist the onslaught of globalisation. 'Our culture', they say, 'is ancient, and has survived for millennia.' In other words, they can accept all the economic advantages, without forfeiting any of the advantages of traditional society.

The truth, or the limitations, of this view do not appear at the level of political rhetoric. The impact of outside values is felt in the sphere of social and familial relationships. The spread of an ideology of individualism does not obligingly halt at some notional frontier of 'private' life: it pervades everything, driving people apart, disengaging them from ancient bonds of duty and custom. Phenomena recorded in the West unfailingly make their appearance among the new middle class – the separation of families, the assault on kinship, the mobility of lives articulated to a new global division of labour.

This is rarely perceived by the economic beneficiaries of globalisation as having anything to do with the advantages they have gained from the integration of their country into a single world economy. They prefer to see it as a consequence of personal changes (usually for the worse), a decline in a sense of responsibility, failings of individuals. In order to reconcile some of the contradictions of economic advantage and social dislocation, many heroic individuals struggle against overwhelming odds.

Box 12.2 Kamala

The fraying bonds of kinship are not only sad personal stories, although they are this also. Kamala, personal secretary to an executive of an internationally known company, is 43. Unmarried, committed to the care of her elderly parents, she also maintains a high-powered career in Mumbai. Her brother is a university lecturer in Houston. Other relatives are scattered all over India. Her mother has Alzheimer's, and her father a heart condition.

Her mother cannot be left alone. When Kamala is not working, she spends her time tending the old lady, who can do nothing for herself. During the day, her father prepares meals, and takes care of his wife's needs.

> What I dread is my father becoming incapacitated. He was a government employee, and has his pension. Money is not the problem. My brother provides everything we need, except his presence. We could buy in care, but I cannot think of strangers with rough hands pulling my mother around, mistreating her. How can you trust such people with the care of someone who cannot even express her needs? At the same time, I cannot give full attention to what is demanded of me at work.
>
> But the thought of staying at home all day, every day, the unrelieved bleakness of what I feel is my duty – I cannot think of it. I love my work. I am efficient and highly regarded. But I wake up in the night when my mother is sick, or she cries out in her sleep. I share a room with her, never sleep deeply. I am always listening for her.
>
> I stayed at home, pursued my career, and thought little of marriage. If you stay with your parents, you still think of yourself as a child, not fully grown up. Then suddenly it is too late. You

are pierced with regret and a sense of loss. The
satisfactions of duty are sometimes overrated,
especially in a society that has become as selfish as
ours. We used to be part of an extended family, but
they have gone their separate ways. Business,
work, professions – money – pull you in different
directions; and there is no going back.

Source: personal communication.

The other middle class

It would be as wrong to think of the middle class as a homogeneous entity, just as it is an error to conceive of 'the urban poor'
as a single block. There are, of course, many middle classes ('the
middling classes' as they used to be called in early industrial
Britain), among them those who have recently risen, by means of
education or enterprise, from the former poor. In an earlier generation, these people would have been in the forefront of the independence struggle, reading Marx and Fanon, and committed to
revolutionary change. The children of this generation are more
likely to be committed to education, social work or NGOs, determined to help the poor in practical ways, once freedom from
colonial rule has been gained.

Many of the third generation since independence have been
absorbed by personal ambition: studying in Europe, the USA
or Australia, rising in an international career structure,
perhaps in transnational companies or in UN or other global
bureaucracies. Some are involved in government administration, and many more in the opening up of former state-run
enterprises to private interests. A considerable number enter
the media – television, films, publishing, advertising and

promotion. There remain, however, a considerable number caught up in NGOs, aid agencies and the voluntary sector. It may be that such people no longer entertain the grandiose visions of their forebears who spoke of transforming the world; but their commitment and dedication to the unfortunates of development, the bypassed and marginalised, are not inferior to those of an earlier generation.

However, the presence of many good people within the new middle class does not alter the overall thrust of their overall economic function, which is to expand spatially and claim a rising proportion of resources.

The priority of a mobile middle class

The most significant rearrangement of urban spaces in favour of the middle class has been the centrality of private transport, which has altered landscapes more than any other single factor.

The ability to go wherever the individual desires is written into the scenario of globalisation. It has become, in the 'developed' world, a human right, and must therefore be transmitted to the locations of privilege in the whole world. In the process, the motor car has become more than fetish: it is literally a cargo cult. Chrome and metal, design and form, speed and movement have become an extension of the human personality itself. Mobility: escape, running away, the chase, avoidance, taking off, moving on, elsewhere, distant destinations – this is no mere functional thing, it is a metaphor of transcendence.

Only in a few thinly populated places of the world can the freedoms promised for infinite mobility be achieved. With the concentration of people in megacities, limitations are severe – not only in congestion and pollution, but also in demands on the public purse for infrastructure to keep up with the volume of traffic. A second major cost is excessive mortality on the roads. The system disadvantages the frail, the old, the sick and disabled. Add to this corruption and irregularities in issuing licences, lack of regulation of working hours of truckers and private drivers, and the folly of giving priority to individual road transport becomes overwhelming. The spread of HIV/AIDS by truck drivers is more than a grim metaphor.

The motorcar is the supreme engine of development. The private car intensifies profound social inequalities, embedding a sense of superior caste or class in those who own one. It permits the rich to avoid a majority of people in their own society, seeing the poor from their vehicles only as importunate beggars miming hunger, selling trinkets or exhibiting their mutilations at traffic lights. Vehicle owners ensure resources will be used to accommodate them on the roads, as a priority over provision of nourishment, clean water, education or health care to the poor. Private cars carry forward into the modern world ancient patterns of prejudice, discrimination and exclusion.

The ambiguities of success

On of the most economically successful cities in the world – and one of the fastest-growing – is Bangalore in the south Indian state of Karnataka. A centre for IT, biotechnology research and knowledge-based industrial innovation in India, it is also a major location for outsourced customer call centres for Western transnationals.

The knowledge industry itself may be regarded as the third great revolution of the industrial era. The first possessed itself of human hands, the manual labour that fed mills, mines and factories of early industrialism. The second revolution captured the human heart – the expansion of professions providing health, education, social care and welfare, which developed with the setting up of the welfare state in the West and in the Communist countries, and which accompanied affluence in the South. The third has appropriated the human brain, locking up knowledge in forms to be released only by those who have the key.

Everybody knows that Bangalore represents India's future. A city developed on a strong industrial base and a wealth of scientific and technological institutions, Bangalore has tempted back more than 30,000 professional people of Indian heritage from all over the world. Most are IT specialists returning from the USA, but there are many other professionals too – lawyers, doctors, academics. Many have come to give something back to their homeland. Others express a desire to return to traditional Indian values. Some acknowledge that living in luxury is easier in Bangalore than in California or Australia. Most have US passports, and many have left their children in the USA for the sake of their education.

All the people are supposed to benefit from the new Bangalore. Extravagant 'farmhouses', gated communities, resorts, gardens, golf courses and pleasure grounds have had a significant impact upon the price of land, already rising under pressure from infrastructural projects – an airport, industrial parks, roads and shopping malls. The IT miracle has indeed touched the lives of most people in Bangalore, but not to universal advantage, as its enthusiasts claim. It is acknowledged that some people have been bypassed by the hi-tech revolution; more rarely is it conceded that others are impoverished by it.

Anita Ratnam works with Samvada, an organisation which encourages science–spirituality dialogues. She works in schools and colleges, encouraging young people to understand the social transformations which are also occurring under an apparently neutral scientific revolution:

> What is the effect upon the psyche and personality of young people in call centres who learn to speak a different

English and pretend to belong to another culture? Too little attention is given to the consequences of what everybody assumes must be beneficial to everyone. Although the IT sector claims to be completely without caste or class bias, it is obvious that the upper castes become upper class and the lower castes lower class. People in call centres are drawn from people with social capital, education and good English, not children who left school at 10.[3]

I met Vinod, whose perfect command of English has earned him a place in a US credit company. He spends his nights in conversation with indebted people from Texas to California. I am the first native English speaker he has ever met face to face. What surprised him most? He said, 'You are not angry like the other people I talk to.'

There are 80 rural districts around Bangalore, in many of which village life has been degraded. Four thousand acres have been designated for the new international airport; more than the operating area of Heathrow, the busiest in the world. Karnataka Industrial Area Development Board over-acquired land cheaply, much of which has found its way into the possession of corporate entities – IT, biotech, pharma and other knowledge-based industries. The airport has led to the growth of floriculture units, since roses and carnations can now be flown to the international flower market in Amsterdam within hours of being picked.

The development of Bangalore has had consequences that reach deep into the rural hinterland. In the rural districts, there are hundreds of men between 25 and 40 who cannot find brides, because no girl wants to marry a farmer. There were 700 suicides of farmers in the four years up to 2006. 'Girls would rather wed a peon in an office earning 3000 rupees a month' (US$75), says Pandurang Hegde, a forest activist from north Karnataka.[4]

A survey into farmers who have sold land has shown that it is mostly small, lower-caste farmers who have sold.[5] Barely 30 per cent of the proceeds have been invested. People have spent money on a daughter's dowry, a television, DVD, refrigerator, a Maruti car. Many have never seen so much money, and have had no experience of handling it. There are no stories of poor farmers becoming multi-millionaires. They have been persuaded by 'brokers' that there is no future in farming, and this has encouraged them to sell. In any case, farmers are under pressure, since in recent years structural adjustment programmes have raised the demand for land on which to produce export goods which earn foreign exchange. The best their children can hope for is to become labourers in floriculture or servants in the resorts and leisure parks.

The corporate sector and its workers pre-empt the best of everything – locations for living, work and leisure – and their money-power procures them the best local produce. This raises the price for everyone else. 'The Corporation used to provide water standpipes in the slums', says Rajendra, who works with Janashayog, one of the few NGOs concerned with urban poverty.

> But now that priority must now be given to privileged incomers, public taps have been removed. Individuals must apply for private connections at Rs1600 (US$40). Since the land on which many slums were built is not regularised, they also have to bribe local officials. Electricity was provided also, street lights and cheap connections. Private connections must now be paid for at Rs2600 (US$60) with Rs150–200 (US$4–5) a month user charges. The government claims that 26 per cent of people live in slums. We think it is at least 33 per cent, but there are no accurate data. Nobody knows. The knowledge-based industries are constructed on a great deal of ignorance. We have counted 788 slums in Bangalore.[6]

The urban poor work in construction, fruit and vegetable vending, city cleaning, loading and unloading, domestic service, making *bidis* and *agarbatti* (cigarettes and incense sticks), hotel and catering, the garment sector and as security guards. Rag-picking is for the very poor, and children work in small restaurants. These are the traditional occupations of the poor. 'The lower middle-class are now also entering these occupations, marginalising the poor further. There is now even less scope for upward mobility, which is potentially destabilising.'

The myth of the city continues to draw young people, not only from Karnataka, but from the neighbouring states of Tamil Nadu, Andhra Pradesh, Kerala and Maharashtra.

> At 19, I came on the bus from Mangalore to look for work. I sat on the bus station, knowing no one, wondering where I should go. An elderly man came to me and said he would give me 100 rupees if I went with him. He took me to an apartment and raped me. I was bleeding badly. He took me back to the bus station and left me there.[7]

Sugata Srinivasaraju is a writer and journalist with *Outlook* magazine. Dedicated to the Kannada language and the culture of Karnataka, he has closely monitored the changes in Bangalore. He speaks of a new techno-feudalism which has reconstructed older inequalities in the image of global social injustice. There have always been migrants to Bangalore, but now only 35 per cent of the people speak Kannada.

> Government cannot generate employment, so it facilitates call centres and promotes private interests, which become a fig-leaf for its own impotence. The Mandal Commission in 1989 advocated reservations for lower castes in government employment. This was immediately

negated through liberalisation. The hope given to Backward and Scheduled castes that they might climb the government ladder was removed.[8]

With about 6.5 million people, there are 2 million vehicles in Bangalore. A further 700 are registered every day. Bangalore is now more polluted than Delhi. Hundreds of trees of this 'garden city' have been felled for road widening. The city, founded in 1537, cannot possibly accommodate the present traffic without radically demolition and reconstruction.

Here is the paradox, not only of Bangalore, but of 'development' in general. The authorities speak of turning Bangalore into another Singapore. To do so they must eradicate the amenities which drew the hi-tech sector to Bangalore in the first place – its shady thoroughfares, its equable climate, its relaxed life-style, its gentle pace of life, its ancient trees. Its images used to be the flame of *gulmohar,* which has been described as the most colourful tree in the world; the scarlet bells of cotton-silk, the twilight purple of jacaranda, the cascades of bougainvillea. IT is sacrosanct in Bangalore: this is the magic carpet which will waft India across centuries of rural stagnation and backwardness towards a future of progress; but it is a future which depends on the erasure of everything that gave Bangalore its unique identity.

Conclusion

The landscapes of today's urbanising world bear such a striking resemblance to those of nineteenth-century Britain that they offer a kind of reassurance: yes, we have been there. We recognise the pain and the pity of people used up by work, sent from one insecure lodging to another, desperate to find an income that will ensure, at the end of a day's labour, a sufficient meal for a family. We see the same patterns of exploitation, identical artful contrivances of survival, similar ways and means of triumphing over adversity.

It seems reassuring, because it suggests that the people who now toil and suffer will, sooner or later, follow the paths which we have trodden, and will join us somewhere in the more or less secure places we now inhabit: the suburbs and exurban estates, the converted lofts and warehouses of an abandoned industrialism, the disused buildings made over into luxury apartments.

If only it were so simple! If only the poor cities of the world could follow the pattern laid down by the early industrial era in Britain, so that the amenities enjoyed by the people of Birmingham, Manchester or Glasgow could steadily be extended to their sisters and brothers in contemporary Kinshasa, Dhaka or Lima! But the prospect of such 'natural' progress is an illusion. During the nineteenth century, when the ideology of non-intervention produced scenes of degradation and squalor hitherto unknown in human cities, it became obvious that the regulation, control and policing of the abuse of human beings was the only way to end the worst of the injustices and inequalities of the industrial city. Limits to the hours of work, to child labour, to insanitary living conditions, to sub-standard dwellings were achieved by legislation. This was fought for by the collective organisations of the poor, and fiercely resisted by the defenders of the economic orthodoxy and minimal government. A comprehensive welfare state, health and education services were finally achieved only after the Second World War, after the defeat of fascism.

The governments of the rich Western countries have – despite occasional rhetoric – certainly not abandoned the protections they extended to their peoples, and equally the privileges which enabled them to make such a spectacular advances, both in welfare provision and in standards of living. The protection of certain markets – particularly agriculture – has enabled them to sustain rising standards in the West. Western-dominated institutions, the IMF, the World Bank and WTO, have institutionalised the benefits to the already advantaged. In relation to the South, however, far from advocating the same severe interventions by government agencies to protect the people, to safeguard their livelihood, their health care, educational provision and nutritional status, the same dominant global institutions have insisted upon a return to non-intervention. They demand this of the governance of the countries of the South, with their appalling agglomerations of misery sometimes dignified with the word 'cities'. What the rich countries are not prepared to implement at home they are only too ready to inflict on the weak and vulnerable.

We arrive at the position where the very policies and processes that created the sufferings of early industrialism are being recommended to the poor world, even when all the evidence points to the fact that these were the cause of the impoverishment and dispossession of the poor. In the Western experience, this began to be reversed only when authorities introduced legislation in public health, to limit the hours of labour, to make education compulsory, to prevent some of the most gross and inhumane abuses of early industrialism.

What future generations will make of this epic mis-understanding (some might call it hypocrisy) it is too early to imagine. One thing is certain. The familiar polluted, dangerous landscapes of poverty, inimical to health and well-being in the South today, are not going to respond to policies that are the reverse of those the West found indispensable to lift up its own people out of despair. It is only by more stringent oversight of the irregularities, injustices and inequalities of globalisation by international agencies, institutions and instruments of gover-nance that improvements may be made. Without some such concerted effort, who can say what levels of degradation, sick-ness, disorder and violence might be reached in the cities of desolation which 2 billion people are, within a generation, expected to call 'home'?

There is no aspect of industrial life known to us from the nineteenth century that is not replicated in the contemporary world: child labour, exploitative hours of work, inadequate living conditions, overcrowding, violence against women and children, wholesale evictions and clearances of people from land required for other purposes, rapid rates of urban-isation, insecurity, high child and maternal mortality, a conspicuous gulf between the rich and poor, malnutrition and the adulteration of food.

These continuities are worth elaborating. Here I shall address only one of the most fundamental, the undermining of nutrition by the use of dangerous substances in food. The addition of poisonous chemicals to food in the early nine-teenth century had serious effects upon both individual health and society as a whole. It was also less detectable then, since many of the industrial and chemical processes were new – created by the industrial revolution itself – and had not been fully analysed. Frederick Accum published in 1820 his treatise on *Adulterations of Food and Culinary Poisons.*[1] Among the practices he described were the adding of chalk, plaster of Paris or powdered stone to flour, the use of alum for lightening the colour of poor-quality flour, or the substitution of cheaper potato flour, while ammonium carbonate was used to improve the appearance of bread made with spoiled flour.

Tea-leaves were readily replaced by other dried leaves – ash or elder leaves dried and artificially coloured on copper plates. Used tea-leaves could be treated with ferrous sulphate and dyed Prussian blue with ferric ferrocyanide. Cheese rinds were coloured with vermilion and red lead, and pepper was adulterated by the sweepings of dust from floors. Some people adulterated their own food – crumbs of burnt toast infused in a teapot gave an illusion of tea – but this was less noxious than additives devised by manufacturers, merchants and dealers. Ale and porter (beer) were coloured and flavoured with copperas, quassia, hartshorn shavings, orange powder, caraway seeds, ginger and coriander. Milk was often diluted with water, while pickles (preserved vegetables) were often coloured with copper. Jellies and sweets were contaminated with lead, copper or mercury, to produce bright colours that would attract children. Chicory (itself sometimes adulterated) and ground beans were added to coffee. Coffee grounds were reused, and there was a brisk sale of stale grounds from the kitchens of hotels and coffee houses. Cocoa was altered with flour, sulphuric acid was added to vinegar, while potted meats may have been made from animals that had died from disease. Iron oxide was used to colour sauces.

With the growth of towns, people who had grown and prepared their own food were removed from the last vestiges of food production, and were the more open to being abused. It is said that some urban dwellers came to believe that milk was naturally yellow and refused to drink white milk. White bread was considered to be more pure than brown, while the additives to beer gave people a taste for a more bitter brew.

In Bangladesh in 2005, the question of adulterated foods became a matter of great public concern. In August 2005, shopkeepers observed a two-day strike in protest against mobile courts, set up by government, to test foodstuffs on sale in the shops and markets of Dhaka, and to confiscate adulterated material and fine those guilty of offering damaging food for sale.

The difference over a period of 200 years lay chiefly in an increasing ingenuity on the part of manufacturers, and a wider range of alteration of foodstuffs. Modern industrial processes have been added to older forms of denitrifying and poisoning foods. Apart from high levels of pesticide in cereals, pulses and vegetables, harmful chemicals used to ripen fruit prematurely and the dyeing of pulses and vegetables, the use of formalin to preserve fish was discovered. Sand and crushed rock had been added to grain, and plastic beads added to cereals and pulses. Water was commonly sprayed on grain to increase its weight, and *ghee* (clarified butter) was adulterated with hydrogenated oil and animal fats.

Til (or sesame) and coconut oil had been added to cotton-seed oil, since these are cheaper; agremone, which contains a highly toxic alkaloid, had been added to mustardseeds before crushing. Dilute buffalo milk was being sold as cow's milk, while wheat and semolina were added to milk powder. Used tea-leaves were being resold, dried and mixed with sawdust and other leaves. Chilli and turmeric had been coloured with lead pigment, while brick dust added to chilli blended with the colour. Metanil yellow, which is a carcinogen, had also been added to turmeric. Carboxymethyl cellulose instead of liquid glucose had been added to soft drinks, while an automobile lubricant was found in *jilapi*, a sweetmeat popular at the time of fasting during Ramzan. An animal feed called vetch, highly toxic, was powdered and used in the making of snacks available at fast-food stalls. Sulphuric acid was mixed with hot milk to speed up the making of posset in the preparation of curd, while urea fertilizer was found in bread and biscuit-producing factories, which made the biscuits and bread 'crispy and white'. Textile dye and burnt Mobil oil were also used in bakery products.

There is, it seems, no form of cheating poor people that the poor of Britain in the early Victorian age had not already known. The assumption is that since 'we' have survived it, so will 'they'. This helps, among other things, to reconcile us to the misery of others, to which, in any case, a majority manage to resign themselves with considerable equanimity.

Replicating the past

If the Western system could survive early industrialism and urbanisation, and the creation of some of the most ghastly conditions in which human beings have ever lived on earth; if it could overcome the emergence of a rival ideology that claimed to place its victims at the centre of a global movement of emancipation; if it proved capable of incorporating those who once appeared irretrievably alienated from its values, it seems that the system can cope with anything. The last quarter of the twentieth century saw the rehabilitation of an ideology which had been under attack ever since the early industrial era – the second coming of a form of non-intervention which saw the transformation of the global division of labour. Work previously done in individual countries was dispersed across a single global entity. This ideology, sometimes mistakenly referred to as the 'free market', is imposed with differential severity on the world. Where it works against the interests of the rich world, it is routinely suspended, but it is imposed without exemption the rest of the time.

This is how the megacities of the present day reincarnate the early industrial period, while their prospects of improvement are constrained by the dishonest advocacy by the West of policies it scarcely practices at home.

One of the most astonishing phenomena of the contemporary world has been the creation of new sites of degradation everywhere. They echo the sights that were faithfully recorded by Engels, Dickens, Mayhew, Booth, Jack London and George Orwell throughout the nineteenth and early twentieth centuries. The scavengers on the rubbish dumps of Manila, Mexico City or Delhi recall the children living from the offal of industrial society in Dickens' London. Conditions in sweat-shops throughout Asia and the *maquilas* of Central America call to mind the relentless rhythm of production in the mills of Manchester. The infernal glass factories, forges and metal works of Dhaka and Guangzhou are faithful replicas of the conditions of early industrialism, while the women and girls working as domestic servants and living in attics, cupboards or on balconies in the suburbs of Mumbai, Sao Paulo or Nairobi lead lives of shameful similarity to their long-forgotten sisters in London and New York.

The self-employment to which millions must have recourse on the streets of Kinshasa, Abidjan or Kolkata is in the same occupations as the un- and under-employed of Victorian London. Even the carts of vendors, the baskets and headloads are identical to those recorded by Mayhew on the streets of London in the 1850s. The trafficking in women and children is reminiscent of the clamour around Josephine Butler's rescue of young women from the 'white slave trade', while there are more slaves in the world today than there were at the time of the formal abolition of slavery.

It is claimed that the 'answer' to these difficulties is the creation of yet more wealth. Since so much has been created in the last two hundred years, a continuation of this benign process is presented as unproblematic. Because the rich countries are the originators of the system of wealth creation, they make the rules by which they claim for themselves exemptions not extended to the poor. Progress and prosperity are inscribed into the imagery of global development, which itself holds out a promise that a whole world can be made 'in our image'; a phrase more significant from having been taken from the Book of Genesis.

During the 1980s and 1990s, criticism by NGOs and social critics was directed at the effects of structural adjustment programmes, imposed by the IMF and World Bank as conditions for further loans to poor indebted countries. When evidence emerged that these significantly disadvantaged the poorest, including the urban poor, the IMF and World Bank prioritised 'poverty reduction strategies' as conditions for debt relief, loans and further aid. In consequence, each country was required to produce a paper showing how the poor would be given priority.

However, the World Development Movement, having monitored the policies contained in the poverty reduction strategy papers for 50 poor countries, revealed in September 2005 that nine out of ten poverty reduction programmes still contained an insistence on privatisation and strict fiscal policy (unlike the policies of the USA and UK, which consistently maintain fiscal deficits), while 70 per cent required trade liberalisation.[2] Far from the 'Washington Consensus' of further liberalisation having been 'declared dead' (by James Wolfensohn, former head of the World Bank himself, at a conference in Shanghai in May 2004), the poverty reduction strategy papers differed only marginally from the old prescriptions of structural adjustment.

It cannot be stated too strongly that the historical experience of the West does not offer a comforting pathway to lead the slum dwellers of the South out of poverty. The road we followed has been blocked not only by the revival of the graveyard ideology of non-interventionism (primarily as an export commodity), but in other ways too.

The rich countries grew rich by exploiting the whole world. The 'hinterland' of British urbanisation, for instance, did not merely cover the enclosed common land of Britain and its pauperised rural population, which provided it with raw materials, land and labour. It depended crucially upon a long imperial moment. In the British Empire were a peasantry that could be coerced into the production of cash-crops, and global markets that could be opened up for the consumption of products made in Britain.

The story of the ruin of farmers for the production of indigo or opium, the efforts to destroy superior Indian textile production in the interests of filling the subcontinent with Manchester cottons, is well known. Indeed, many of the small comforts of industrial life which helped to reconcile the labouring poor of the great industrial towns and cities to capitalism were extracted from colonial lands – tea, coffee, tobacco, snuff, cocoa, sugar. The transfer of wealth from poor to rich, the plunder of treasures, gold, silver and works of art from the colonised world, was a characteristic of the colonial period. The cities of Europe were embellished with the wealth seized from elsewhere – the adornment of Brussels from Leopold's Congo, the ornamenting of Madrid and Lisbon from the Americas, the imperial finery of London. They are all symbols of other people's impoverishment and loss.

The overcrowding and misery of the cities of the South pose another practical, though largely unarticulated, question to the world. How could the very developmental patterns which have increased inequality a hundredfold in two centuries be applied world-wide? They have brought our planet the menace of climate change, the effects of 50,000 chemicals in the soil, air and watercourses, the depletion of forests, oil and water, the degradation of the biosphere. What would be the consequences if the other four-fifths of humanity also followed such a course? These epic issues are glided over in the technocratic jargon of international financial institutions and instruments of global governance.

When concerned scientists, moralists and activists raise the issues, they are often met with denial, as when President Bush and the lobbyists of the US energy industry claim the phenomenon of global warming is unproved. Even the eager tokenism of the Kyoto protocol is far from answering the urgency of the hour. At best it will make a only minimal impact on the fate of the world. In any case, the newly industrialising countries – China and India in particular – correctly observe that no restrictions were ever placed upon the West in 200 years of polluting industrialism. Since they are being exhorted to emulate Western development, why should they be expected to curb the by-products of a system from which no departure is now allowed by the dominant powers of the world?

If the only hope for the poor is to follow the familiar path of growth – the ruinous ideology of economic expansion in perpetuity – with the rich benefiting at least as much as the poor, what kind of life would today's already-rich have to gain, if the poverty of the cities and their drained, exhausted hinterlands were to be even slightly mitigated?

The cities pose these questions in the most stark material form. If chaotic and uncontrolled urbanisation is perceived as a potential catastrophe, this is because there is no guarantee that the resources, the wealth, or even the capacity, exist for the planet to bear the raising up of all the people of the world. The work of slum improvements, of livelihood, of security of tenure, the labours of NGOs, charities, self-help groups, popular movements – all the mobilisation of 'civil society' – are fine and noble endeavours. But they provide no coherent plan, no blueprint, not even the outline of a solution that will accommodate, not merely the existing inhabitants of slums and informal settlements, but also the hundreds of millions to be added to them in the coming decades.

Other forms of intervention, more imaginative kinds of governance, less corruption – yes; but equally, another form of development is needed, which depends less on material resources and more on human resourcefulness. How might human societies disengage from a mechanistic delivery of economic growth, which is spread so unevenly, and far from lifting people out of poverty, only conjures new forms of poverty out of the very wealth it creates? Different definitions of poverty, other concepts of wealth are called for. The need is not for capitalism, rigged markets (or even some mystical notion of completely 'free markets) to spread world-wide, but for more humane alternatives. We need to present definitions of what constitutes human well-being. We need to quantify the costs of development which pollutes, spoils and lays waste the earth, the species and the societies it bears.

A world in denial is ill placed to do what is necessary. It is not for the oppressed and the powerless to say what must be done to mitigate what privilege has wrought. As *The Challenge of Slums* suggests, if the present course of (in)action continues, the excluded will certainly create more disorder than anything we have yet seen.[3] There will be more illegal economic activity, more violence, more quarrels over resources if everything is left to the ambiguous mercies of the dominance of markets, whether these are biased in favour of the rich, or genuinely 'liberated' after the fashion of those of early industrialism.

If the excesses of poverty in the slums, tenements and cellars of Victorian Britain were capable of reform, this depended, to a considerable degree, on an imperial capacity to mine the resources of a wider world. That wider world is now urged to follow the same path, but without the vast hinter-lands to open up, to explore and to annexe for people's well-being. In the process, developing countries are also being required to do away with the kind of protection for the poor that became essential, in the name of both humanity and social peace, in Britain. They are caught between two intolerable pressures.

This is the real challenge of the slums. It should not be business as usual in a limitless commitment to economic growth, but the provision of a secure sufficiency for all on earth. This was an ancient dream of humanity, which is as far away today from being realised as it was when it was first conceived in the misty dawn of our human consciousness of justice.

Resources

Themes: urbanisation, globalisation and cities, slums, rural–urban migration, urban inequalities, urban life, organisations.

Bibliography

The following books are recommended reading for those interested in a more in-depth coverage of the issues presented in this guide. Each focuses on a particular sector of the urbanising world, and provides an overview of the topic in question as well as further resources and a complete bibliography. The books range from theoretical to very practical, allowing for diverse intents on the part of the researchers.

Abbott, John, *Sharing the City: Community Participants in Urban Management*, Earthscan, London, 1996.

Amen, Mark, Archer, Kevin and Bosman, M. Martin (eds) *Relocating Global Cities from the Center to the Margins*, Rowman & Littlefield, Lanham, Md, 2006.

Burgess, Rod, Carmona, Marisa and Kolstee, Theo (eds) *Challenge of Sustainable Cities*, Zed, London, 1997.

Devas, Nick and Rakodi, Carole (eds) *Managing Fast Growing Cities*, Longman, Essex, 1993.

Fernandes, Edesio and Varley, Ann (eds) *Illegal Cities: Law and Urban Change in Developing Countries*, Zed, London, 1998.

Gilbert, Alan and Gulger, Josef, *Cities, Poverty, and Development: Urbanization in the Third World*, Oxford University Press, Oxford, 1992.

Hurley, Donnacadh, *Income Generation Schemes for the Urban Poor*, Development Guidelines series, Oxfam Publishing, Oxford, 1990.

Mukhija, Vinit, *Squatters as Developers*, Ashgate, Hampshire, 2003.

Nando, Christina and Coetzee, Erica (eds) *Urban Vulnerability Perspectives from Southern Africa*, Oxfam Publishing, Oxford, 2002.

Neuwirth, Robert, *Shadow Cities: A Billion Squatters, a New Urban World*, Routledge, London, 2006.

Potter, Robert B. and Lloyd-Evans, Sally, *The City in the Developing World*, Addison Wesley/Longman, Essex, 1998.

Todaro, Michael P. and Smith, Stephen, *Economic Development*, 9th edn, Pearson Education, Essex, 2006.

UN-HABITAT, *The State of the World's Cities: The Millennium Development Goals and Urban Sustainability*, Earthscan, London, 2006.

Publications/web resources

The following publications and web resources include statistics, databanks, reports, background papers, journal articles and basic informational sources, categorised by chronological topic relating to the chapters of the guide. Many of the listed references are intended as a starting point for further research, highlighting a particular organisation's wealth of resources or singling out a particular issue of a journal or magazine which focuses on urbanisation-related topics.

Urbanisation

SASI and Mark Newman, World Mapper (2006)

http://www.worldmapper.org/

This is a useful and interesting website for gaining perspective. World Mapper displays maps with the territories sized in relation to the subject mapped, on a variety of subjects including urban slums, services, debt services and population. All data is reliably sourced.

UN Development Programme, *Human Development Report*: 2006 data

http://hdr.undp.org/hdr2006/statistics/

Link to the statistics used to produce the *Human Development Report*. This is an interactive site with access to the data for all the indicators used in measuring human development, many of which are directly related to urbanisation and urban life. A recent addition to the site is the ability to customise a table with individually selected indicators, which facilitates isolating and comparing relevant data.

UN-HABITAT, Habitat Debate Vol. 12, No. 3, June 2006

http://www.unhabitat.org/pmss/getElectronicVersion.asp?nr=
2104&alt=1

This issue of *Habitat Debate* provides an overview of the issues discussed at the World Urban Forum (Vancouver 2006). It is presented from the UN point of view, with commentary from UN-HABITAT experts.

UN-HABITAT, World Urban Forum

http://www.unhabitat.org/categories.asp?catid=41

Links to a record of all the documents from the three World Urban Forums (2002, 2004, 2006) including pre- and post-session documents, World Urban Forum Sessions reports, and speeches. This information is useful for a general synopsis of urbanisation and the current issues being discussed by governments and NGOs, as well as for an introduction to the key international players (both organisations and individuals) in the work of alleviating urban poverty. These forums address both developed and developing country urbanisation issues, the most recent with a focus on sustainability and local action.

World Bank: Urban Development, 2006

http://web.worldbank.org/WBSITE/EXTERNAL/TOPICS/EX
TURBANDEVELOPMENT/0,,menuPK:337184~pagePK:149
018~piPK:149093~theSitePK:337178,00.html

A section of the World Bank website with discussions, event listings, publications, background papers and topic summaries of a number of related subjects, including urban services to the poor, urban environment, urban poverty and urban health. Publications and papers from the World Bank tend towards a strong Western, neo-liberal, pro-privatisation approach.

World Bank: *World Development Report*

http://econ.worldbank.org/WBSITE/EXTERNAL/EXTDEC/E
XTRESEARCH/EXTWDRS/0,,contentMDK:20227703~page
PK:478093~piPK:477627~theSitePK:477624,00.html?

While not focused specifically on urbanisation, much of the information provided in the *World Development Reports* is directly related to urbanisation as more and more of today's developing countries urbanise. These documents are most useful for the compendium of indicators which accompany each report, which complement rather than duplicate the statistics in the Human Development Report.

World Health Organization (WHO): The urban environment

http://www.who.int/heli/risks/urban/urbanenv/en/

A general reference for policy and research regarding the effect of urbanisation on the environment and the health of individuals.

This is an overview but contains a number of links to more detailed information on specific health risks. This site also contains a directory of international NGOs working with WHO on research, civil society and policy creation with reference to a healthier urban environment.

Globalisation and cities

Douglas, Mike and Boonchuen, Pornpan, 'Bangkok: intentional world city', in M. Mark Amen et al. (eds), *Relocating Global Cities from the Center to the Margins*, Rowman & Littlefield, Lanham, Md, 2006

Narrative and academic, this chapter narrows in on the economic decision behind becoming a global city. Though primarily a treatise on the relationship between finance and city planning, the chapter also touches on the consequences of these decisions for the urban poor, including slum dwellings, lack of public amenities, and the compartmentalisation of urban spaces.

Eldis

http://www.eldis.org/globalisation/index.htm
An online knowledge base for the development industry, with a supply of constantly updated material such as resource guides to available tools in the field as well as full-text articles and country guides. This particular section focuses on globalisation, but there is an equal amount of resources available for issues such as water and sanitation, and poverty. The selected resources are aimed at researchers and policy makers, but cover a wide spectrum of viewpoints and concepts, and include links to supporting documents and websites.

Environment and Urbanization (April 2002)

This issue of *Environment and Urbanization* focuses almost exclusively on the changing landscape of cities in a global world. It includes case studies of developing cities as well as discussions of the types of mechanisms required to ensure that a city continues to account for the needs of its citizens.

Tyner, James A., 'Labouring in the periphery: the place of Manila in the global economy', in M. Mark Amen et al. (eds), *Relocating Global Cities from the Center to the Margins*, Rowman & Littlefield, Lanham, Md, 2006

A theory-based article which approaches the concept of globalisation as a result of a deliberate reshaping of space. Using Manila as a case study, this chapter outlines a number of themes related to economic globalisation and how it works out in urban spaces. Issues discussed include urbanisation and employment policies, globalisation, and global city formation.

Slums/informal settlements

Houghton, Suze (dir.), *On the Map*, 2005, 8 minutes

http://www.cohre.org/view_page.php?page_id=252
A documentary about insecure housing and slum conditions in which over half of the 2.5 million inhabitants of Indore (India) live. The film covers the difficulty of building livelihoods when living in fear of relocation, but finishes with the positive story of an innovative local organisation bringing changes in the communities through upgrading and other methods.

Payne, Geoffrey, 'Getting ahead of the game: a twin track approach to improving existing slums and reducing the need for future slums', *Environment and Urbanization*, Vol. 17, No. 1, April 2005

A practical look at achieving the Millennium Development Goal No. 7, improving the living condition of 100 million slum dwellers by 2020. Using a case study from Cambodia, Geoffrey Payne explores intermediate tenure options as a reasonable solution to a difficult problem. The approach to the article is straightforward and it is set up as a step-by-step to understanding the problem and the potential solutions.

Smolka, Martin, 'Informality, urban poverty and land market prices', *Land Lines*, Vol. 15, No. 1, January 2003

http://www.lincolninst.edu/pubs/PubDetail.aspx?pubid=721
A general analysis of land policy in Latin America and the resulting informal land market. Simply written, this is a very broad overview which gives insight into the push for regularisation and its failure to address the basic issue of the cycle of urban poverty.

UN-HABITAT, *Habitat Debate*, Vol. 5, No. 3, 1999

A response to the adoption of the Habitat Agenda in 1996, this issue of *Habitat Debate* covers the various aspects of informal settlements and insecure tenure. A number of countries' policies are brought under the microscope, including South Africa, Bangladesh, India, Brazil and Western Europe.

Rural–urban migration

Development Resource Centre (DRC) on Migration, Globalisation, and Poverty

http://www.migrationdrc.org/research/typesofmigration/
internal_migration.html
The DRC, based at the University of Sussex but active in five countries (the United Kingdom, Bangladesh, Albania, Egypt and Ghana), provides a resource base for documentation, publications, and key projects concerning migration, including internal, forced and skilled migration. The DRC's main aim is to influence policy rather than to engage in on-the-ground activism. It also aims to support the field through publications and seminars.

Overseas Development Agency (ODA) 'Internal migration, poverty and development in Asia', briefing paper, October 2006

http://www.odi.org.uk/publications/briefing/
bp_internal_migration_oct06.pdf
A short discussion of the importance of temporary internal migration on the reduction of rural poverty. This paper includes a brief background of the impetus for internal rural–urban migration as well as the risks to the migrants and the benefits to the economy.

Paling, Dennis, 'Development induced forced migration: a practical example', *Development in Practice*, Vol. 10, No. 2, May 2000

A case study of a peri-urban settlement between Izmet and Istanbul which was displaced by the expansion of the city. This article follows the paths of the displaced individuals, discusses their loss of livelihood and increased vulnerability. Although academic, this article still offers a 'slice of life' portrayal.

Urban inequalities

Fernades, Edesio, 'The influence of de Soto's *The Mystery of Capital*', *Land Lines*, Vol. 14, No. 1, January 2002

http://www.lincolninst.edu/pubs/PubDetail.aspx?pubid=199
This article is one of the more academic included in this resources section. It focuses on ideologue Hernando de Soto's book *The Mystery of Capital*, its proposals and ideas, and the practical result of many Latin American countries practising what de Soto preaches.

International Seminar on Segregation in the City, 26–28 July 2001, Cambridge, Mass.

http://www.lincolninst.edu/education/
education-coursedetail.asp?id=83

Papers produced for this seminar are available online and deal primarily with urban inequalities, in both developed and developing countries, and the resulting urban spaces. They look at how inequalities divide cities socially and economically, and create a fear of the other. Of particular interest is Glenn Pearce-Oroz's paper, 'Causes and consequences of rapid urban spatial segregation: the new towns of Tegucigalpa' (http://www.lincolninst.edu/pubs/dl/611_pearce-oroz.pdf), which incorporates the theme of urban spatial segregation in a framework of forced internal migration and the resulting rapid urbanisation.

Rakodi, Carole, 'Planning for whom', in Nick Devas and Carole Rakodi (eds), *Managing Fast Growing Cities*, Longman, Essex, 1993

This is a unique attempt to educate planners on the perspective of the urban poor. Written as an entreaty to the technical profession, this chapter outlines the difficulties of informal housing and informal livelihoods. It also offers a brief history of how the informal sector has been perceived by society. Most useful is a comparison between traditional and responsive urban planning, including a number of useful principles and processes.

Urban life

Ali, Mansoor (ed.), *Solid Waste Management as if People Matter*, special part issue of *Habitat International*, Vol. 30, No. 4, December 2006

This issue of *Habitat International* includes a collection of accessible articles focusing on issues in waste management in the informal sector. Written by practitioners, the content includes a great deal of good practice, lessons learned and practical examples. The topics range from recycling and waste reclamation to government challenges to the role of the private sector. Each contribution provides an introduction to relevant stakeholders.

Amos, Jim, 'Planning and managing urban services', in Nick Devas and Carole Rakodi (eds), *Managing Fast Growing Cities*, Longman, Essex, 1993

This chapter is highlighted because it manages to convey the issues from a planning standpoint without being unduly technical. It begins with a practical discussion of urban services, what they are, and the context in which they are intended to be implemented. It also stresses the interdependence of the various aspects of the physical infrastructure (water, sanitation, roads, electricity), and how this poses problems when the rate of urbanisation far exceeds the ability of the infrastructure to keep up.

Mooya, Manya M. and Cloete, Chris E., 'Informal urban property markets' *Urban Studies*, Vol. 44, No. 1, January 2007, pp. 147–65

http://www.gla.ac.uk/urbanstudiesjournal
Heavy on economic theory, this article uses new institutional economics to create a framework linking informal settlements and the alleviation of urban poverty. After outlining the theory, Mooya and Cloete lay out the necessary conditions that need to occur in order to successfully use informal settlements as a tool for improving living conditions. They also provide a comprehensive literature review and propose a future research agenda.

Organisations

Asian Coalition for Housing Rights (ACHR)

73 Soi Sonthiwattana 4
Ladprao 110, Ladprao Rd
Bangkok 10310
Thailand
http://www.achr.net/index.htm
A group based in Bangkok, ACHR first developed out of a meeting of regional housing NGOs in response to an eviction situation in Seoul. It engages in organising hands-on grassroots activity, and also produces housing rights-based publications (such as A *Decent Place to Live* by Denis Murphy). Its most successful action to date is a Training and Advisory Programme (TAP) which organises regional involvement. The website includes a great deal of information about both ACHR and partner projects, as well as general regional information in the field of housing, and country contacts for nearly every country in Asia (http://www.achr.net/asia_focal_points.htm).

Centre on Housing Rights and Evictions (COHRE)

COHRE International Secretariat
83 rue de Montbrillant
1202 Geneva
Switzerland
http://www.cohre.org/index.php
COHRE is a Netherlands-based NGO, focusing first on advocacy, training and education as regards housing rights and legal issues, and second, on monitoring, documenting and preventing forced evictions. COHRE works with partner organisations in both the developed and the developing world. It has a strong legal component, and directs resources towards litigation and legal advice for communities involved in housing campaigns.

Community Organization Resource Centre (CORC)

http://www.courc.co.za/
This group is a resource for grassroots activists as well as professionals, and serves as a network for urban and/or poor communities. CORC is intended to be a resource for learning, with action as the ultimate aim. Founded in 2002, it has begun a number of professional support programmes geared specifically to the urban poor. Since 2005 it has widened its reach to include rural and peri-urban communities, and has narrowed its focus to green and brown development issues. Despite these changes, CORC continues to support partner organisations like CUP (Coalition of the Urban Poor).

Chronic Poverty Research Centre

University of Manchester
Harold Hankins Building, Booth Street West
Manchester M13 9QH
UK
Tel: (+44) (0)161 275 2810
Fax: (+44) (0)161 273 8829
http://www.chronicpoverty.org
Affiliated to the Overseas Development Institute (www.odi.org.uk), the Chronic Poverty Research Centre was established in 2000 as a cooperation between universities, NGOs and multilateral agencies, with the intent of influencing policy through research and analysis. This site provides a number of reports and publications on the topic of chronic poverty, many involving urban settings.

International Institute for Environment and Development (IIED)

3 Endsleigh Street,
London WC1H 0DD
UK

Tel: (+44) (0) 20 7388 2117
Fax: (+44) (0) 20 7388 2826
email: info@iied.org
http://www.iied.org
This organisation's focuses are climate change, governance, natural resources and human settlements. Its work, focused on urban poverty, includes taking part in research consortia, influencing donors and promoting micro-finance. The IIED website has a link to a media room whose purpose is to provide up-to-date information on a spectrum of environmental and urban issues. This organisation also publishes the journal *Environment and Urbanization*.

International Organization for Migration (IOM)

17 Route des Morillons
CH-1211 Geneva 19
Switzerland
Tel: (+41) 22 717 9111
Fax: (+41) 22 798 6150
email: hq@iom.int
http://www.iom.int
IOM is an inter-governmental organisation which advises on policy and promoting orderly international migration. Much of the research conducted, however, takes into account labour-induced internal migration as well as the effect of remittances on national development. IOM also engages in activities that involve health, rights and gender-based migration.

Practical Action

The Schumacher Centre for Technology & Development
Bourton on Dunsmore
Rugby CV23 9QZ
UK

Tel: (+44) (0) 1926 634400
Fax: (+44) (0) 1926 634401
http://practicalaction.org
A development agency with a bottom-up approach, which
works in Latin America, Africa and South Asia, Practical
Action's current agenda regarding urbanisation is to lobby for
the inclusion of the impoverished within the Habitat Agenda.
It campaigns for good governance and secure housing as well
as water and sanitation issues, pursuing an integrated
approach for physical infrastructure. The website is a good
source of information, in particular regarding urban services,
for which it gives access to technical briefs and to a resource
centre of documentation relevant to development.

Save Bombay Committee

Prakruti and Save Bombay Committee
102 MAUSAM Co-op Housing Society
Plot No. 285, Sector-28
Vashi, Navi Mumbai 400705
India
Tel: (+91) 22 27899699
http://www.savebombaycommittee.org/
An organisation created in 1973 in Mumbai in order to
struggle for the improvement of quality of life, the Save
Bombay Committee has expanded to work across the country, at both a national and a local level. Some of its activities
are providing guidelines and development assistance to
governments as well as lobbying for government agencies to
be created and then playing a role in their creation. The
organisational priorities are decongestion of slums, improving minimum health standards, water and sanitation,
sustainable, pedestrian-friendly transport, as well as a
number of ecological initiatives.

Slum Rehabilitation Authority

5th floor, Griha Nirman Bhavan
Bandra (E), Mumbai 400051
India
Tel: (+91) 22 26590519/26590405/26591879/26590993
Fax: (+91) 22 26590457
email: info@sra.gov.in, gharkul@sra.gov.in
http://www.sra.gov.in/

A government authority, based in Mumbai, and established in 1990 with the purpose of managing slum rehabilitation. All residents of Mumbai who have resided continuously in a slum since 1995 and who form a committee representing at least 70 per cent of the slum population are eligible for rehabilitation. This site is very useful in terms of understanding the government perspective on slums and efforts to rectify the situation. This authority's site provides information on the stages of slum rehabilitation as well as a listing of all its current projects, along with contact details, location and the individuals working on those projects. For certain projects there are also links to plans, current and projected layouts.

Society for the Promotion of the Area Resource Centres (SPARC)

2nd floor, Khetwadi Municipal School Building
1st Lane, Khetwadi, Girgaum
Mumbai 400004
India
Tel: (+91) 22 23865053/23858785
Fax: (+91) 22 23887566
http://www.sparcindia.org/

An NGO based in Mumbai, SPARC began in 1984 by working with pavement dwellers. It is now a national organisation which works in partnership with the National Slum Dwellers

Federation and a network of women's cooperatives to provide access to housing and infrastructure. Its activities are varied, ranging from putting on exhibitions of affordable housing and sanitation resources for government agencies, to working with micro-financing. SPARC also works to encourage learning between communities, and sets up pilot housing projects to demonstrate the possibility of providing low-cost but secure housing.

UN-HABITAT: United Nations Human Settlements Programme

PO Box 30030, GPO
Nairobi 00100
Kenya
Tel: (+254-20) 7621234 (Operator)/7623120 (Information Services Section)
Tel: (+254-20) 762 3151/3153 (Media and Press Relations)
Fax: (+254-20) 7624266/7624267/7624264/7623477/624060
email: infohabitat@unhabitat.org
http://www.unhabitat.org
The mission of this UN agency is to provide 'sustainable urban development and adequate shelter for all'. Its projects focus on advising policy makers as well as local communities in accord with the UN Millennium Declaration, in particular the target to improve the lives of slum dwellers by the year 2020. This volume of the Small Guides to Big Issues series draws heavily on a UN-HABITAT report from 2004, *The Challenge of Slums*. The UN-HABITAT website is a primary source for reports, projects, brief updates and documentation concerning human settlements worldwide.

Notes

Introduction

1. UN Human Settlements Programme, *The Challenge of Slums*, Earthscan, London and Stirling Va., 2003.
2. Gordon McGranahan, Pedro Jacobi, Jacob Songsor, Charles Surjadi and Marianne Knellen, *The Citizens at Risk: From urban sanitation to sustainable cities*, Earthscan, London, 2001.

Chapter 1: An urbanising world

1. Jorge E. Hardoy and David Satterthwaite, *Squatter Citizen*, Earthscan, London, 1989.
2. Brigitte Overtop, Oxfam Netherlands, www.oxfamamerica.org.
3. The 'Green Revolution' involves attempts to dramatically increase agricultural production by using single-crop agriculture with improved varieties of seed. It usually requires high usage of water, fertilizers and pesticides.
4. UN Human Settlements Programme, op. cit.
5. Juan Ferero, *New York Times*, October 2004.
6. Adam Nicolson, *Guardian*, 13 February 2006.
7. Ravi Sundaram, *Economic and Political Weekly*, 3 January 2004. Sarai, Centre for the Study of Developing Societies, New Delhi.
8. See sieresources.worldbank.org/INTEAPREGTOENVIRONMENT /Resouces_Huai_river-pollution_EN.doc.
9. Marcel Henaff, 'Vers la ville globale: monument, machine, reseau', *Esprit*, March-April 2004.

Chapter 2: Cities of the past, cities of the present

1. Friedrich Engels, *The Condition of the Working Class in England in 1844*, George Allen & Unwin, London, 1952.
2. Henry Mayhew, *London Labour and the London Poor*, London, 1851.
3. *Chetai*: panels of woven bamboo.
4. John Reader, *Cities*, Heinemann, London, 2004.
5. Import substitution is the policy of trying to reduce imports (and hence the spending of foreign exchange expenditures) by encouraging the development of domestic industries.
6. The Washington Consensus is a set of policies first presented by John Williamson from the Institute for International Economics in 1989, and subsequently supported by the IMF, World Bank, World Trade Organization (WTO), and many national governments. The policies include the mass privatisation of state-owned enterprises.
7. Leopold Kohr, *The Inner City*, Y Lolfa, Talybont, Dyfed, Wales, 1989.
8. http://en-wikipedia.org/wiki/Bamako. See also World Bank Country Assessment Report, 2002.
9. UN Human Settlements Programme, op. cit.
10. Gillian Tindall, *City of Gold: The biography of Bombay*, Temple Smith, London, 1982.
11. http://en-wikipedia.org/wiki/Cairo.

Chapter 3: The global network

1. Saskia Sassen, 'Losing control? Sovereignty in an age of globalisation,' in *The 1995 Colombia University Leonard Hastings Schoff Memorial Lectures*, Columbia University Press, New York, 1996.
2. Leila Vignal, 'Une metropole des marges de la mondialisation. L'exemple du Caire', *Esprit*, March–April 2004.
3. Globalization and World Cities Research Group, 1999, Loughborough University, UK. http://www.lboro.ac.uk/gawc.
4. Jacques Donzelot, Villes à plusieurs vitesses et économie d'árthipel, *Esprit*, March–April 2004.

5. US Census, http://pewhispanic.org/files/reports/69.pdf.
6. *Guardian*, 22 November 2004.

Chapter 4: Migrants to the city

1. US Census, http://pewhispanic.org/files/reports/69.pdf.
2. www.censusindia.net.
3. www.ennenjanyt.net.

Chapter 5: The spectre of the poor

1. UN Human Settlements Programme, op. cit.
2. Niji Akanni, *Lagos: Love it or Love it*, Sarai Reader 02, The New Media Initiative, SDS, New Delhi, 2002.

Chapter 6: Slums

1. UN Human Settlements Programme, op. cit.
2. Jorge E. Hardoy and David Satterthwaite, op. cit.
3. 'Forced evictions', www.cohre.org. Centre on Housing Rights and Evictions, 83 rue de Montbrillant, 1202 Geneva, Switzerland, 2004. COHRE Media Release – 25th February 2004.
4. See for example http://www.citymayors.com/society/zim babwe_ evictions.html
5. Gita Dewan Verma, *Slumming India*, Penguin Books, India, 2002.
6. UN Human Settlements Programme, op. cit.
7. Mike Davis, *Planet of Slums*, Verso, London, 2006.

Chapter 7: Livelihoods

1. Salathivel Pinaki Jaddar, 'Unorganised sector workforce in India', *EPW*, 27 May 2006.
2. Henry Mayhew, op. cit.
3. Mike Davis, op. cit.
4. Mike Davis, op. cit.
5. *Tehelka*, New Delhi, 2 October 2004.

6. Imran Ahmed Siddiqui, *The Statesman*, Kolkata, 17 September 2004.
7. Siriporn Skrobanek et al., *The Traffic in Women*, Zed Books, London, 1997.
8. Naomi Klein, *No Logo*, Flamingo, London, 2000.
9. 'Profile of the *maquila* apparel industry in Honduras', www.researchandmarkets.com/reports/42912.
10. Personal communication, March 2005. Sarai is a vibrant research and activist organisation based in New Delhi, working on the impact of new media upon the city, city life and images of the city.

Chapter 8: Cities of fear

1. *Guardian,* 18 December 2004.
2. Reuters, 14 October 2004. See also http://news.bbc.co.uk/1/hi/world/americas/3740994.stm.
3. Division for Building Technology, Council for Scientific and Industrial Research (CSIR) and the Institute for Security Studies, 'Environmental design in South Africa', www.iss.co.za/Pubs/Monographs/No16/EnvironmentalDesignInSA.html, accessed 19 March 2007.
4. Rory Carroll, 'Brutal divide: fortified town plays on middle class fear of crime', *Guardian*, 11 February 2006.
5. IIED, *Environment and Urbanisation Brief No. 10*, London, 2004.
6. These are the subject of discussion among international agencies concerned with urbanisation.
7. *Economist*, 19 June 1999.
8. http://www.un.org/ecosocdev/geninfo/afrec/vol15no1/151city3.htm
9. www.cleanclothes.org. Use the search facility to find entries on 'fire'.
10. SNDP Bangladesh. www.sadpbd.org.
11. Colombia Solidarity Campaign. www.colombiasolidarity. org.
12. Basic Needs. http://mentalhealthanddevelopment.org.
13. Joyce Sirimoni, personal communication.

14. Joyce Sirimoni, personal communication.
15. IABAS, New Delhi, 2004.
16. Institute of Human Behaviour and Allied Sciences, New Delhi, 2004.

Chapter 9: Provision of basic services

1. UN Human Settlements Programme, op. cit.
2. Carole Rakodi, *African Towns and Cities: Powerhouses of development or slums of despair?* http://www.uic.edu/ cuppa/cityfutures/ papers/webpapers/cityfuturespapers/session1_2/1_2african.pdf.
3. News Reports, All India, 2005, e.g. www.iht.com/articles/ 2005/07/29/news/india.php.
4. www.unicef.org.
5. 'Lusaka', Suzanne Daley, *New York Times*, 18 September 1998. For Nairobi, see http://streetkids.org.uk.
6. Derek Eaton and Thea Hilhorst, 'Opportunities for managing solid waste flows in the peri-urban interface of Bamako and Ouagadougou', *Environment and Development*, Vol. 15, No. 1, 2003.
7. Ivan Illich, *H_2O and the Waters of Forgetfulness*, Marion Boyars, London, 1986.
8. From Oxfam (2006) *In the Public Interest*, Oxford, Oxfam.
9. UN Human Settlements Programme, op.cit.
10. McGranahan et al., op. cit.
11. Sylvy Jaglin, 'The right to water versus cost recovery: participation, urban water supply and the poor in sub-Saharan Africa', *Environment and Urbanisation*, Vol. 14, No. 1, 2002.
12. Carole Rakodi, op. cit.

Chapter 10: City borders

1. L M van den Berg, M S van Wijk and Pham Van Hoi, 'The transformation of agriculture and rural life downstream of Hanoi', *Environment and Urbanisation*, April 2003.
2. Information from author's visit to Oxfam project, Lucknow, March 2004.
3. UN Human Settlements Programme, op. cit.

Chapter 11: The country and the city

1. Jorge E. Hardoy and David Satterthwaite, op. cit.
2. C. S. Molyneux, V. Mung'ala-Odera, T. Harpham and R. W. Snow, 'Maternal mobility across the rural–urban divide: empirical data from coastal Kenya', *Environment and Urbanisation*, Vol. 14, No. 1, 2002.
3. International Development Research Centre, reported at Canadian Association for African Studies, 1993.
4. Chuma Ezedinma and Comfort Chukuezi, Comparative analysis of urban agricultural enterprises in Lagos and Port Harcourt, Nigeria.
5. Paul Jenkins, 'In search of the urban–rural frontline in postwar Mozambique and Angola', *Environment and Urbanisation*, Vol. 15, No. 1, 2003.

Chapter 12: The triumph of the middle class

1. Saskia Sassen, op. cit.
2. *The Making of the English Working Classes,* Gollancz, London, 1963.
3. Anita Ratnam, interview with author, 2005.
4. Pandurang Hegde, personal communication, 2005.
5. Anita Ratnam, awaiting publication.
6. Rajendra, personal communication.
7. Personal communication to author.
8. Sugata Srinavasaraju, personal communication. See also http://www.freeindiamedia.com/jeremy/18apr_2005.htm.

Conclusion

1. Accum, a German chemist living in London, was the first person to expose these practices; his book was an immediate best seller.
2. World Development Movement, www.wdm.org.uk.
3. UN Human Settlements Programme, op. cit.

Index